# The Pet Sitter's Tale

## LAURA VORREYER

authorHOUSE®

*AuthorHouse™*
*1663 Liberty Drive*
*Bloomington, IN 47403*
*www.authorhouse.com*
*Phone: 1 (800) 839-8640*

*Published by AuthorHouse  12/06/2017*

*ISBN: 978-1-5462-1328-4 (sc)*
*ISBN: 978-1-5462-1326-0 (hc)*
*ISBN: 978-1-5462-1327-7 (e)*

*Library of Congress Control Number: 2017916049*

*Print information available on the last page.*

# Dedication

With deep appreciation to my family and
friends for their love and support.

And for Dexter, my canine soul mate.

# Gratitude

Thank you to all my wonderful clients who befriended me and treated me like family. Without your trust, I wouldn't have been able to spend precious time with the pets that I came to love so dearly.

With gratitude to all the fans that follow me on my social media accounts especially on Twitter @PetSittersTale. Several of you sent pictures of your dogs for the book and I tried to use as many as I could. In fact, all of the dogs pictured in the book are client's dogs, friend's dogs or came from social media and I thank you all sincerely for giving me permission to use them. Dexter, of course, is my dog and he gave me his permission in exchange for treats. The pictures of Dexter, both by himself and with me were taken by Charlie Nunn at Charlie Nunn Photography here in Los Angeles. Charlie Nunn and Raymond Janis graciously donated these pictures for use in "The Pet Sitter's Tale" and I cannot thank them enough. Look them up (www. charlienunnphotography.com). They take the best pet portraits!

Like so many other people, I've had my share of ups and downs these last fifteen years, especially during 2007-2010. I am extremely grateful to my loyal base of clients that never abandoned me and continued to use my service despite the now plethora of dog walking and pet sitting options available. During some of my darkest days, the only thing that got me motivated enough to leave my bed were the pets that waited for me.

I'd especially like to thank my brother John and his family for their generous support and compassion while I was going through a particularly bad time.

As an active dog walker I spent many hours in solitude with the dogs, hiking in the hot, summer sun of the San Fernando Valley. It is during one of those walks that I bent to pick up dog poop and the bag seamlessly broke, leaving me picking up poop with my bare hands. (Insert vomit emoji here.) In addition to immediately reevaluating my life choices, I also had a great idea: there should be wet wipes on dog poop bag dispensers.

Having already been contemplating my future, and giving serious thought to what could be my next business move, this sudden inspiration was an "Aha" moment for me. I became obsessed with this concept, (bags and wipes combo) and literally clung to the hope that I could get the product to market even though I knew nothing about inventing, manufacturing, patents, production costs or any of the other stuff someone has to know to successfully bring a product to life. Without any money, to boot!

Not knowing how to proceed, I took my sister's advice (thank you, Raine!) and enrolled in a *Life Mastery* course here in Los Angeles, with Jay Levin. This course absolutely helped me change my life and I am so glad I took it. If there is anything I can share here (without taking too much time), it is this: Move forward towards your goals everyday, even if it's a tiny step. Make one phone call, send one e-mail, join a group, do something, do not let one day go by without moving forward towards the life of *your* dreams.

Everyday I took this advice and I eventually transformed my own reality. While working on the invention I also took time to join a writers group, which is something I always thought I would like. I was explaining my new life philosophy to a writing group friend and she summed it up nicely by saying, "Inch by inch, life's a cinch."

While I wouldn't agree that getting a product to market is a cinch, it's anything but. I do think that breaking monumental tasks into smaller more manageable tasks is an effective strategy. Another effective strategy? Believing in magic. The magic of the Universe and that the Universe is conspiring in *YOUR* favor. You can manifest your own destiny!

Wanting to continue on my journey of self-improvement I discovered and subscribed to Mike Dooley's, *Notes from the Universe*. Mike's program and TUT Notes (The Universe Talks) gave me daily encouragement, optimism and motivation. Thank you, Mike!

I came to the realization and understanding that we are, all of us, the entire universe. We're made from stars and we're here for something amazing and it is anything we want it to be. I studied the *Law of Attraction* and shifted my own beliefs and perceptions about myself. I stopped telling myself I was "just a dog walker" and remembered that I am an entrepreneur, too. I stopped seeing my own life through the filter of other people's success. I forgave my parents, let go of negative thoughts and found a better, more supportive tribe for myself.

With each day I was more determined to move from entrepreneur to inventor and in 2012 I met my boyfriend (now husband), Larry, who helped me more than any one person get the product to market. In September of 2014 we stood proudly, side by side, and launched our product, the Doggie Doo All together in Chicago at *The Total Pet Expo*.

All during the time Larry and I were getting to know one another, I told him pet sitting stories and he said, "You should write a book." The thing is, I had written some of these stories down but had chosen to pursue the product because I wanted to give it all my energy and remain singularly focused. I lived and breathed the product; it was an obsession of mine.

After the product was launched, I revisited some of the stories I had written and began to revise them and edit them trying to make them readable and entertaining. After I had written and re-written these tales several times I sent them off to my fabulous editor Keidi Keating at Your Book Angel. Keidi polished the book up better than I could have ever hoped; she really is a book angel.

Thank you, Keidi!

People are truly crazy about their furry children, especially since they don't steal our credit cards and crash our cars.

I humbly present this book to you, the reader. It has been over fifteen years in the writing. I have so many other stories I could tell but choose to protect the innocent and prevent any negative feelings from anyone. I changed the names and mixed-up the circumstances in these stories. I purposely did not match the dog's picture before the story so no affiliation to a particular dog or client could be made.

If this book inspires you, makes you laugh or even just love your pets that much more, then I have done my job. Please adopt a dog (or two) from you local shelter and foster a pet in need, if you can. Always remember to treat animals with the love and kindness they deserve and teach your children to do the same.

If you like the book, drop me a line at Laura@thepetsitterstale.com

And if you don't like it, scream it into your pillow and keep it to yourself.

With many thanks and woofs!

Laura Vorreyer
Los Angeles, California
August 15, 2017

# Contents

Juno

# There Will Be Poop

During career day in the fifth grade, a teacher asked, "What do you want to be when you grow up?" I remember thinking, "a grown up," duh. I was dying to escape my childhood. It never crossed my mind on that particular day that I wanted to be a pet sitter or a dog walker. In fact, I'm pretty sure these positions didn't even exist way back in 5th grade. I remember thinking I wanted to be a lawyer. I found out later how much school was involved to be a lawyer and that put me off. I was always waiting for lightening to strike and suddenly just know the exact educational and career path to take in order to fulfill all my dreams. At one point, while I was a teenager, I was convinced I wanted to be a news anchor. Not a journalist but an anchor, someone who sat on camera and read the news, looking good while doing it. Something glamorous but intelligent at the same time.

I don't know why but I let my mother convince me that news anchors have to get up really early which is not something I did well. Many years later, I found myself working at the cosmetic department in Barneys New York Department Store, selling foundation to a woman whose 27-year-old daughter was a news anchor in Texas, and the mother could not have been prouder. I was 32-years-old at the time.

I felt compelled to do something with my life that would capitalize on what I did well. My parents, especially my mother, tried to convince me to learn how to type perfectly as that would be my ticket to a

1

better life. Become an excellent typist, be a secretary, get the boss to fall in love with me and then, problem's solved. My mother had been my father's secretary and it had turned out well for her.

I never did learn how to type proficiently, despite four years of it at an all-girls Catholic High School in Chicago. I never broke 47 words a minute with 33 errors. I was a terrible typist then, and in fact, I still am. I look at my fingers while typing, spell-check is my religion, and I will die believing hunt and peck is the fastest way to go. Once, while trying to temp my way through college, I had to take this horrible typing test. On the appointed day, I felt so anxious about the test, I wrapped one of my fingers with a Popsicle stick and some medical tape and told the test administrator I had sprained my finger. I was a bit surprised when she asked me how I had sprained my finger. However, I find that preparedness is key, especially when trying to get a temp job that pays eight bucks an hour. I told this nice lady that I had sprained my finger walking my dog. Well, dog lovers of the world unite! Wouldn't you know it, she had a dog too, and boy, could he pull hard when he got going! She sent me on an interview for a position downtown in the investment field, taking my word that I could in fact type 95 words a minute, and I landed the job. I am nothing if not resourceful.

Thankfully the position only required light typing, and I managed to have most of it accomplished before anyone could notice or care how long it took.

Telling this story about my dog, King, really saved my ass, but in fact, it couldn't have been farther from the truth. From the very first day my mom brought King home from the Anti-Cruelty Society, the name had already gone to his head. He didn't go for walks.

But before that, there was Ginger. Ginger is the earliest memory of my unhappy childhood. I remember playing with my brother on the carpet in our dining room. It was probably 1972. I was 4 years old. Our house was a stuccoed bungalow on the north side of Chicago in a working-class neighborhood full of policemen, firefighters, and city workers. We had multicolored, shag carpeting in weird, abstract patterns you couldn't make sense of. The blues faded to darker blues and even black but then other blues got lighter and faded to a lighter color and then to white. We had this carpet in the living room and dining room. Thank God, my mother had the good sense to do our bedrooms in solid colors. Navy for the kids' rooms, rust for hers and Dad's.

I was playing with my brother, who is two years older than me. We were playing with "Lincoln Logs" or "Tinker Toys." My sister would have been napping at this time. She is two years younger than me. It was late afternoon. My father came through the front door with this small, black furry bundle. He put the bundle down on the floor and it ran over to us, my brother and me. It kissed us and licked us and made us shriek with laughter. I was instantly in love. And I have been ever since.

Fast forward to 1980 when I was twelve years old. My mother was determined to punish me by prohibiting any of my family to speak with me. I am a pariah in my own house. I sat in my bedroom by myself, staring at the fake wood paneling while sitting on my mustard yellow, corduroy bedspread waiting for my mother to come in and berate me. She would work herself into a fury, and finally, when she couldn't take it anymore she would beat me. I stood in the doorway of my room, not allowed to leave the threshold of this doorway. Ginger was in the hallway having a nap. "Ginger," I whispered, "Ginger, come here." She raised her head and looked at me. She trotted into my room and sat down wagging her tail and staring at me. "I love you, Ginger," I said. She was my only friend.

Every pet I have taken care of since then is Ginger. I look into all of their eyes and see the liquidy soulful eyes of my best friend. I cannot repay the debt of kindness and the loyalty Ginger demonstrated to me. I can only hope to do right by her by taking care of each and every animal as if it were my own.

Hannah

# Going Pro

Hordes of people come to Los Angeles every year to become rich and famous. As unremarkable as that is, I was no different. In 2002, I moved from Chicago to Los Angeles to work in film and television as a makeup artist. I had a clear plan of what I would do when I arrived in LA and had taken action steps to secure a job in my field. I was fortunate enough to work at Barney's New York in Chicago as a makeup artist, and had the floor manager at the Chicago store recommend me to the floor manager at the Barneys in LA on Wilshire Blvd.

My intention was to work at the makeup counter at Barney's while I figured out the lay of the land and then somehow brake into film and television. Looking back, I should have worked on the "somehow" part more. At the time of my move though, I was concerned with navigating Los Angeles and adjusting to life outside of Chicago. I had been born and raised in Chicago and had spent my entire life there. I knew nobody in Los Angeles but had always felt I wanted to live there, even though I had only visited once. After spending most of my adult life in corporate sales, I had gone back to school to be a makeup artist in my early thirties and had started getting jobs right out of school. There was no reason to think that a transition to working in Los Angeles would be that difficult.

I landed at a cosmetic line on the West Coast Barney's floor called

Cle de Peau. Loosely translated, it means Key to Beauty. Cle de Peau is Shisheido's luxury line. Supposedly all the makeup used in *Moulin Rouge* was Cle de Peau. We didn't carry this line in Chicago so I had to gain some expertise and education about it because unlike the counters I worked at in Chicago, this counter had a sales quota. The sales quota was pretty high, around $650 per day. I wasn't too worried about the quota though, because I didn't plan on sticking around.

The artists were all waiting for their big break and I was the same. No one was overly concerned with their numbers. We all realized that at any moment, we might break through. We were all simply killing time at the counter until something better came along.

The other women who worked with me were beautiful and young. Impossibly young, they looked like children, only taller. I overheard a twenty-three year old tell her friend she had been getting Botox since the age of seventeen and would die if she ever got any wrinkles. Youth is the god of this town.

I was certainly a fish out of water, already in my thirties and desperate to get out of retail and into film and television. I subscribed to hotlines, talked to agencies, and networked but nothing was coming of it. I was running out of money quicker than I could have imagined and I was seriously worried about my future. I picked up some wedding work through inquiries made at the counter but nothing that gained any traction.

I upped my game and started to build a career as a makeup artist. I reached out to photographers hoping they would partner with me and do some Trade for Prints (TFP's) where you provide your service gratis and the photographer gives you the choice of prints you want for your portfolio.

I was living in Burbank and connected with a photographer in Culver City. He called me on a Tuesday afternoon and asked if I was available to do makeup for a model later. An artist had cancelled so he could use the help. I studied my *Thomas Guide* to see how far apart Culver City was from Burbank. They were on separate pages of the map book but this didn't worry me. Nothing would stop me. This was before navigation systems or smarty-pants phones. It was just me and a book of maps called the *Thomas Guide*. I liked to call it the *Doubting Thomas Guide* because I am bad with maps and directions.

I spruced myself up, grabbed my kit and portfolio, and eagerly drove to Culver City. It was easy enough to find and I pulled up outside the photographer's studio on Venice Blvd. with plenty of time to spare. As I was waiting in my car, a strawberry blonde in a red convertible parked across the street and went inside. *Ah, the model,* I said to myself and followed close behind.

The shoot went according to plan. She was pretty with gorgeous skin and we did some natural shots for her book, followed by some more glamorous shots. There were a couple of wardrobe changes but nothing too major. We finished at around 6 p.m. and the model left. I cleaned my brushes and chatted with the photographer, Guy.

Guy was from back east, but he had lived in LA for a few years. Guy was packing up his equipment and sprucing up his place. It turned out he lived and worked there. He sat on his couch and asked me if I wanted to smoke some pot with him. I am no pothead but I figured, *what the hell, I'm a grown woman and I can smoke a little pot?* Besides, I could hear the traffic from the passing cars below and didn't feel like sitting in it.

Guy and I smoked a bowl together and I started picking his brain about the industry.

"Got a union card?" he asked me. I was so surprised by his question that my first thought was, *what union?* I didn't have a union card and didn't even know there was a makeup artist union. I told him I was from Chicago and the union wasn't an issue there. He told me I wouldn't get any work on any film and television jobs while I didn't have my union card. Shit, I hadn't known this. This new information disturbed me and suddenly I didn't feel like getting high with Guy, so I left.

I got back in my car figuring I could wing it back to Burbank because I had arrived here okay during the daytime, but now it was nighttime and I ended up at the ocean.

The ocean and Burbank are not even close to each other. Then I wrongly concluded that the PCH would take me to Burbank and I almost ended up in Santa Barbara. I pulled over to consult my maps guidebook only then realizing I had left my portfolio at Guy's. I was trying not to panic but I was feeling pretty panicky anyway. There was no one I could call. I now had another task: getting my portfolio back. And I had just learned I had to be in the makeup artist union to get any real work.

I felt so anxious I couldn't concentrate enough to make out the map book. I couldn't figure out how to get back to Burbank. I drove further up (down) the coast and stopped at a gas station. I asked the attendant to please give me directions to Burbank, and he tried to sell me the *Thomas Guide*. "Just give me a hint," I said. "I'm not from around here." Finally feeling some sympathy for me, he told how to get back to Burbank, and it took two hours.

Back in my utility apartment I ate ramen noodles and plopped into bed. I had to be at Barney's early in the morning. The Barney's employees and vendors had to go in through the basement where their personal things were stored in a locker. Personal items had to be placed in a clear bag so the guards can see any contraband. We stood in the queue in the basement with our tampons, condoms, and drugs on full display. I loved working at Barney's, despite it being demoralizing.

I couldn't afford to buy a thing but I wanted all of it. It was excruciating. The people who came in were either already wealthy or wealthy from being in the industry. Not only were they buying the things I wanted, they also worked at the jobs I coveted. After a while the riches became oppressive and I realized the emptiness in it all. I tried to appreciate and focus on the concept of non-duality, which basically means that since it even exists, it belongs to all of us. This is a Buddhist teaching, which is almost impossible to apply at a very materialistic LA store.

The fact that I made it to LA at all and was working in Beverly Hills had given me a sense of pride when I first arrived but I had been here a while by now and nothing was happening. At first, there was no feeling equal to walking into Barneys New York on Wilshire Boulevard in Beverly Hills. It was intoxicating to me. The smell of the perfumes, lotions and potions, candles, and the beautiful people who would pick them up and admire them… everything was amazing. All possibilities existed inside Barney's. Now, the walls were closing in.

The next day, I was standing at the counter again bright and early as the doors opened. The women came in first. All dressed to the nines with their luxury handbags that cost more than my car. I smiled politely at them and even said hello to some of them quietly. No one said anything to me.

The girls at the next counter giggled loudly when a man came in and said, "Good morning, ladies." They were each so exquisitely made up, they could be store mannequins.

It is against Barney's rules to fix your makeup at the store counter but there are mirrors everywhere so you can't help but look. I noticed my reflection and saw that what looked like the perfect amount of blush in my crappy apartment lighting is more the perfect amount of blush for a clown and not at all the right look for Barney's. I crouched down and tried to wipe away some of the damage when from the corner of my eye I saw a little dog circling behind a couch.

I noticed a young woman, the dog's owner, looking pitifully distressed. The dog was winding up to lay it down and there was no stopping the train. "Oh shit," said the woman. I popped up from the behind the counter as if on cue and walked over to her. She was mortified. I told her it was okay; Barney's had that effect sometimes.

The dog came running over to say hello and I bent down and petted the dog and told her she was a naughty girl doing her business inside Barney's. The dog was friendly and very excited.

The good people at Barney's let you bring your pets in but if your pet did its business there then you were on your own. Unless you were Lindsey Lohan, and then they would wipe your dog's ass if you wanted them to.

I quietly explained to the woman, Amanda, that she had to clean up the mess. She looked as if she was about to burst into tears. During all of this I was trying to keep my eye on my counter. Amanda didn't have any clean up supplies with her so I told her to go to the washroom and grab some paper towels and that I had plastic garbage bags at the makeup counter.

I was trying to be helpful to this poor young woman and her dog, Abby. Abby was so cute and I brought her back to the makeup counter. She was a terrier of some kind, black and white and fluffy, and about twenty pounds.

Amanda cleaned up but had to run outside to throw the poop out, which took a while. I was beginning to wonder if she had gone to Santa Monica to toss the poop bag when my boss, Lolly, approached me. She didn't like me and immediately asked why I had a dog at the counter. I told her that the dog didn't belong to me, that I was only holding it for a client, and she told me to get rid of it. Now.

Finally, after what seemed like an eternity, Amanda came over to the counter extremely grateful that I had helped her. I handed her back Abby who was behaving really well on her leash. "Oh hey," said Amanda, "are you a makeup artist?"

"Yeah, I am." I told her all about Cle De Peau and how they used it in Moulin Rouge and she bought some eye shadows, which I hoped Lolly saw so I'd get some credit for making a sale.

Amanda asked me if I would do her makeup for a low budget independent movie she was starring in. She told me about the movie and her role and that it would involve aging her a bit. She said she would pay me out of her own pocket. It was only for a few days but she could introduce me to the director and producer and maybe something would come of it. The movie was shooting next weekend in Santa Monica, and she asked me if I was interested. I told her yes, I was pretty thrilled.

Amanda left as Lolly was walking to the counter with the store manager to rat me out for having a dog at work. "Good thing you had your friend pick up your dog," said Lolly.

"You can't have dogs at work," said the manager.

"She isn't my dog." I told them, she was a customer's dog.

"Uhm hmm," said the floor manager, not believing me. "I'm giving you a verbal warning. The next time it'll be in writing, and then after that you'll be terminated. Do you understand?" I nodded while Lolly squinted her eyes at me.

Lolly was an aging beauty queen. She was only friendly with the male makeup artists. She showed open contempt for most of the majority of woman who worked in the shop, apart from the managers, who naturally, she was best friends with.

"You'd better make your quota today," Lolly said and turned to walk away in the same direction as the store manager. *She's probably going to go and give him a blowjob now.* The girls across the store snickered and stared.

I should probably explain why Lolly didn't like me. It could have been one of a few reasons, besides her general dislike for any other woman.

First, Lolly wasn't given the chance to interview me for the open position at her makeup counter, though, this was not my fault, it didn't prevent her from holding it against me. When I moved from Chicago to Los Angeles, the managers at the two stores had simply worked it out for me. I understand that from Lolly's perspective, this undermined her authority and maybe she had a chip on her shoulder about it, just a theory.

The second reason Lolly didn't like me was entirely my fault, I admit, we got off on the wrong foot. I'm confident now that Lolly would have never given me the job if she had met me before my employment was arranged.

The first day I met Lolly and the other artist I was a nervous wreck. The week before I had done an anonymous dry run through the store to get my bearings and while I tried to remain inconspicuous, everywhere I went somebody asked me if I needed help. Desperate to remain anonymous, I gave everyone and everything the side-eye, refused to speak and didn't buy a thing. If Barney's had had a bouncer, I would have gotten the boot.

Walking through the cosmetic department, I can see the artists are having an impromptu meeting of sorts. I approached them and felt anxious and awkward. Some of them were wearing those maddening lab coats giving them an authoritative air. They formed a semi-circle around Lolly, the high priestess, nodding their heads to whatever she said. I slowed my pace, my internal anxiety panel about to explode. I had plenty of time to take in their short skirts, stilettos and tan legs. Why hadn't I taken the time to spray tan my own legs? I could have at least shaved them this morning? As I closed in, the scent of their collective perfume overpowered me and I started to cough.

I approached the group to introduce myself, keeping my breathing shallow so my cough would not turn into a full on hack. I tried to say something charming and funny. I stood there waiting for a lull in the conversation so I could chime in.

Finally, they all turned to me, this stranger standing around trying desperately to act like I fit in. I was a deer in the headlights, literally blinded by what I saw. Each one of them was stunning and they all had the most enormous breasts I had ever seen. Every pair unique but equally mesmerizing; breasts with colorful tattoos, breasts with long gold chains dangling from them, breasts perfectly contoured and bursting out of half unbuttoned silk shirts. Clearly I shouldn't have been concerned with going to work showing too much skin. It was all a bit much.

"Holy boob-jobs!"

How could I not comment on something that was so obvious? Everyone knew I was being sarcastic, come on, that was sarcasm at its finest! Back in Chicago, sarcasm was a currency we all traded in so I thought this would be hysterical. Looking back now, I don't know what I was thinking. The artists gasped and tittered, clickety-clacking their way back to their own territories.

"Hi," I said to Lolly, immediately trying to move past what had just happened. She narrowed her eyes, shooting invisible daggers my way. I wanted to take it all back but it was too late, that was strike two.

I busied myself at the counter after the dog incident and noticed that one half of my face still had the clown blush. I made the necessary adjustments to my face as the floor manager walked by again. He saw me adjusting my makeup and shook his head. I gave him my best smile. The counter was not busy this morning and I glanced around to make sure no one was looking before calling Guy. I wanted to get my book back so I left him an urgent message to call me. I had been looking for makeup work and applying for jobs. I felt sure something would pop soon and the gig with Amanda was a good start. "Something always leads to something," I said to myself. However, this isn't necessarily true because sometimes, something leads to nothing and then you are right back where you started. But I wanted to stay positive.

I managed to get an interview out in Chatsworth with a movie studio making "adult entertainment films." Porn, I know, but I needed the money and I felt like the job at Barney's was on thin ice.

Later that afternoon, an elderly looking woman came in wanting her makeup done. We offered complimentary makeovers at the counter and once our product was skillfully applied a client would usually purchase at least one or two items. Sometimes out of guilt, but nevertheless, a sale is a sale.

The woman slid into one of the makeup counter chairs and sighed. "Make me look younger," she said.

I laughed and said "Scalpel," holding out my hand like a surgeon.

This would have been hysterical in Chicago but this woman failed to laugh.

I emphasized her eyes and complimented her on their beautiful color; I gave her lips extra attention and made them look moist. "A moist lip is very youthful," I said to her. We finished and she left, then Lolly immediately strutted over.

"Mrs. Crabdath didn't buy anything?" she asked me.

"Uh, not today," I said.

"Well, why not?"

"I don't know."

We stood at the counter staring at each other. My feet were killing me. I wondered how these young girls wore stiletto's all day. I was in wedges and my feet felt like they were going to fall off. I wondered if the other girls took painkillers in order to wear their high heels all day. I was going to need to get my hands on some.

I hoped Oprah would come into this Barney's. Just seeing her would make me feel better, and I would view it as a positive sign from the Universe. Oprah used to come into the Barney's in Chicago all the time and she really lit the place up. An Oprah sighting was like seeing a shooting star. I suddenly missed Chicago and felt like I had made an awful mistake thinking I could come to Los Angeles and be a makeup artist.

As if I didn't feel bad enough, Lolly told me she was taking me off the schedule for the rest of the week as she had too many artists at the counter. I still had to stay until closing though. I exited through the basement after the embarrassing check through of all my personal items. I then got in my VW Beetle and took my shoes off; I had blisters all over my feet.

I went home that night and cleaned my brushes and polished my little palettes. MUDD the makeup school was right down the street from where I was staying and a bunch of international students were down at the pool.

"I heard there are more makeup artists than actresses here in LA," one said while guzzling her homemade margarita. They were laughing and drinking and jumping in and out of the pool.

"It's no laughing matter," I said to no one in particular and closed my sliding door. I pulled out my laptop and looked at my dwindling finances. I was dangerously close to being completely broke. Next month's rent would be due soon and I didn't have it. I glanced around the room for things to sell but saw nothing. I dialed Guy's number again and left him a message; I still needed to get my portfolio back or I wouldn't be able to show my work.

For the next couple days I sent e-mails and made calls. I managed to schedule one appointment to apply make-up for a wedding, or "dreadings" as I now called them.

I had made friends with another makeup artist from Chicago. Lisa was industrious and resourceful and I admired her. She had developed a business designing themed princess parties for poor little rich girls in Beverly Hills who wanted nothing more out of life than to be a Disney Princess.

"Lisa," I said to her, on our way to the first one, "I'm slightly rattled about creating this princess look for these little girls. I'm not sure what they're looking for, and I don't want to let them down."

"Oh", Lisa said, "don't worry about that, just whore them up." We took turns taking swigs of vodka from a flask she kept in her glove box before going inside. Tiny Belles and Jasmines greeted us all wanting fake lashes and colorful lips. The moms were equally delighted to see us and left us alone so they could drink Bellini's and Mimosas. Lisa and I spent the next two hours applying makeup to their flawless little

16

faces as they all asked for "more, more!" At the end of the party we presented the girls to the moms who took pictures and told us how wonderful we were.

Lisa went to the kitchen to collect the money as I cleaned brushes and scraped lash glue off my makeup case.

Once we got back in the car Lisa gave me $500 cash.

"Oh wow," I said, "Lisa, you don't have to give me all of it. Let's split it."

"That is splitting it!" she told me. I was grateful for Lisa's generosity but I realized these gigs were few and far in between and I needed a steady gig with a steady paycheck.

Friday finally arrived. As I got dressed I considered what it might be like behind the scenes of a porno shoot. I wasn't too interested in finding out but the money was really good. I told myself to just go and see, and if it wasn't for me then I didn't have to accept the position.

I dressed all in black but tied a red scarf around my neck. I wanted to look professional but not too prim. I hoped I didn't look like I worked at a Mexican restaurant. I took the red scarf off and put on a leopard print one. The leopard print one matched my wheelie, my makeup kit on wheels. *Hmm, too matchy-matchy*, I thought. I was deliberating then realized I had to go so I went down to my Beetle with my wheelie. I didn't have my portfolio anymore and I felt empty handed. I had emailed them my resume and had gotten the call off of that. I packed my wheelie into the backseat and got in. *If they ask me about my portfolio what am I going to say?* I thought about this all the way to Chatsworth. I could say it was stolen, which was looking like the truth, but it seemed unlikely. I could say I lost it but again that seemed unlikely. I could just say I forgot it, but that seemed like stupidity on my part. In the end I decided to tell a terrible lie that I'd left my portfolio on a plane and the airline had lost it. Airlines are always losing things, right?

I drove my car on the 118 Freeway to Chatsworth. I had never been on the 118 before. There were lots of firsts in California and I was trying to cherish all of them. My first time on the 118 Freeway, followed by my first time on the set of a pornographic movie, go me. I'm crushing it out here in LA.

On my arrival I noticed that the house wasn't just a house, but more of a compound of houses. A guard came out of a little guardhouse and asked me my name. I told him my name and that I was there for an interview. One of his eyebrows shot up.

"Makeup artist interview," I clarified. Apparently, I don't look like I can be in a porno.

"Main house," he said and nodded in the direction of the biggest house, the one in the middle. I drove in and noticed expensive cars parked everywhere.

I parked my Beetle under a tree offering the tiniest bit of shade. I didn't know if I should bring my kit in or not. The house had some stairs leading up to it and the wheelie could be unwieldy.

"Bring it!" I said to myself. "You don't have your portfolio, but at least you have your freakin' kit." Besides, it was a million degrees and the thought of all my makeup turning into puddles was unacceptable so I pulled my kit out of the car by its expandable handle. I was a little more self conscious of the print matching my scarf now that I was wheeling towards the door but told myself, "You're your own brand. You're representing your brand and you match and that's okay."

I took a deep breath and knocked on the front door. A woman in a bikini bottom with bare breasts opened the door, I was getting used

18

to the sight of breasts at this point so it was easy to act unfazed. "Hi," she said and looked at me tilting her head. "Hi," I said back, not looking at her breasts. "I'm Laura, I'm here to interview with Artie."

"Yup," she said, starting to lead me away from the door and inside the foyer.

We walked down a long hallway towards the back of the house. Lights and cameras were set up in various rooms but nothing was being filmed as far as I could see.

"We're on lunch," she said, reading my mind. The house was spacious and cool and the hallway was carpeted. I was grateful for that, because my feet were a mess. The house was well-appointed, even rich looking, and I was comforted by the fact that this was apparently a top of the line porno-making company. There were awards mounted to the walls showing various gleaming plaques and trophies.

The woman in the panties stopped at double doors at the far end of the house, which were opened to an office with mahogany furniture, red carpeting, and nicely framed movie posters.

A rotund man sat at a desk but didn't get up when I came in. "Here she is," the woman said as I went through the doors.

"You're the makeup artist?" he asked.

"I am," I said and extended my hand across the desk to shake his. "I'm Laura, it's so nice to meet you."

"Is it?" he shot back.

I wasn't sure what to say to this so I said the first thing that entered my mind. Well, maybe the second thing because I had learned my lesson from my humiliation at Barney's.

"Congratulations on all your success."

"Success? This is success?" He stared at me with beady eyes.

"Well, sure," I say, hoping to win him over with my Midwestern charm. "You're certainly at the top of your game. I noticed all your awards on the way in."

"Ah," he said, "you know what that is? That's hard work."

"Absolutely!" I said.

"So," he said, "You want to be a makeup artist?"

"I *am* a makeup artist," I said, emphasizing the word "am."

"Right, right," he said.

My wheelie was sitting to the side and I nudged my head towards it as if to demonstrate my credentials. I would kill Guy if I ever saw him again.

"What's your name, hun?" he asked me. I don't think he had ever interviewed anyone with their clothes on. I told him my full name.

"L.V.! Your initials are L.V., like Las Vegas," he said excitedly. "I love Vegas!"

"Yes!" I said back enthusiastically, "and like 'Louis Vuitton,' too!"

There was a long bout of silence before Artie remembered he was conducting the interview. He asked me if I could come up with "one more thing that has the initials L.V.?" and he'd give me a crack at the job.

I looked around the room quickly. I felt like Kevin Spacey in *The Usual Suspects*.

I glanced at the poster above Artie's head. I noticed that the poster had been hung in such a way that from where I was sitting it looked like Artie's head was in the poster scene and he was about to receive two loads of ejaculation from beefy men with their erect penises pointed at him. It was one hell of an optical illusion and I had to hold back a snicker.

I looked away from the distracting poster and glanced around the room.

*LV, LV, LV, what else has the initials LV?*

"Lottsa Viagra!" I shouted out. I burst it out like a game show contestant running out of time to solve the winning word puzzle.

We both laughed. Artie gave a hearty chuckle.

"Okay kid, we'll give you a try for the rest of the day and see how you take to it."

"Okay great! Thank you very much for the opportunity."

"Sure kid."

I got up and grabbed my wheelie and walked out into the hallway. The woman who had been topless earlier was now wearing a tight sporty tank top with the number 69 on it. Nothing was subtle; it was all in your face, just another day at the office.

"Come with me," she said, "I'll show you around."

I followed her around while self-consciously pulling my wheelie.

She took me into various rooms used as sets. It was definitely someone's house and I wondered if it was Artie's. Maybe he lived here with his family? I tried to imagine him eating Thanksgiving dinner in the house with his family but couldn't. I looked into all the rooms and then we went into the kitchen area. "This is the kitchen," she said to me, which was obvious, but I nodded my appreciation for her having pointed it out anyway. "Have a seat," she said and I pulled out a chair and sat down. She asked me if I wanted something to drink but I declined.

"We usually order in for lunch," she said, "but feel free to bring your own food and use the fridge."

"Sure," I said. "Thanks."

"You've got to label stuff though. If you don't label it, it's anyone's."

"Okay," I said. Who knew that working in porn would be like working anywhere in corporate America?

"You're not from LA, are you?"

This was quickly becoming my least favorite question. She hopped up onto the kitchen counter and positioned herself across from where I was sitting, her pussy looking right at me.

Suddenly I needed a beverage, but one with alcohol, however, this was an emergency and anything would do. I stood up, walked to the fridge, and grabbed a can of diet coke. I opened it and took a drink. I hated when people assumed I wasn't from LA.

"Chicago," I told her. "You?"

"Alabama."

"Oh, I've never been to Alabama…"

"Neither have I. That's my name."

Of course it was. Why shouldn't she have a name like Alabama or Madison or even Detroit for that matter? I'm sure it wasn't her real name, that was a stage name, and her real name was irrelevant. She could call herself whatever she liked.

"I'm Laura," I said.

"I know" she replied, and rolled her eyes. "Where did you go to makeup school?"

"Columbia."

"Oh. In New York?"

"No, in Chicago."

She asked me about my education and work experience. She wanted me to tell her exactly how I was qualified to work there, with her. She was interviewing me because she was the talent. The star.

I took her questions seriously and answered thoughtfully. I told her about all my experiences working on various videos, theatre projects, and films.

She asked me if I can air brush and I told her I can but I didn't have my own machine.

She jumped off the kitchen counter, spun around, yanked up her shirt, and showed me her backside. It was quick, so it took me a second to realize exactly what was happening. Once I saw it, there was no unseeing it.

I looked at her butt and considered all the actions I had ever taken to wind up there in this exact moment in time and space staring at her rear end. Obviously, wrong choices had been made. Clearly there were times when I zigged and I should have zagged. And just like that, I knew this experiment of mine, giving the porn shoot a chance, was going to come to an end.

It's one thing to have your dreams of stardom crushed but it's quite another to have them crushed by ass acne, which our star had in spades.

"Can you cover this?" she demanded. I studied her posterior while simultaneously contemplating if any amount of therapy would eradicate this memory.

Alabama/Madison/Detroit's butt was covered with pimples and scabs and discoloration scars where pimples once were. There were fading black and blue marks below each of her cheeks in the shape of fingers.

I knew I didn't want the job. I really, really didn't want the job.

I didn't know what to do. I couldn't stand the idea of touching this woman's butt or using any of my makeup brushes on her pimply behind. I stared at her ass trying to decide if this was just acne or maybe some sort of venereal disease, when suddenly, another one of the "stars" walked in.

Alabama/Madison/Detroit slid back up on the kitchen counter. One thing was certain; I would starve to death before I ate anything that came out of this kitchen.

"Hey," he said to the star, while giving me a wink, "don't scare her off just yet."

"Too late," I said weakly, "ha, ha."

I wanted to make my escape but couldn't imagine doing it with any dignity if I had to drag my wheelie behind me. For an instant I considered abandoning it.

"Did you get the script notes for the next scene?" he asked me.

"There's a script?" I wondered aloud.

"Ha!" He laughed at me. "You're not from around here are you?"

Fuck. The rest of the day went by slowly. I dedicated one and only one of my makeup brushes to the job, a big, flat, squirrel-haired brush, which I used with the broadest of strokes to camouflage the catastrophe. After I applied the concealing foundation, Alabama/Madison/Detroit set it with a huge puff she dunked in baby powder. The resulting clouds, made me gag.

I decided that as soon as I got home I would pour bleach on the brush and *then* throw it out.

Naturally, the movie we were working on had some inane name, like *Indiana Bones* or *The School of Cock*.

Alabama/Madison/Detroit was playing herself. The scenario was that she had enrolled in a music class to learn how to play the guitar but the instructor had another instrument in mind. Oldest story in the book.

In between takes Alabama/Madison/Detroit told me she can, "really play the guitar." I had stopped speaking to her altogether.

Apparently there was no other makeup to do. She did her other makeup herself and I got to do her butt. I was beyond miserable. I took off my scarf and tied it around the handle of my wheelie. The pattern was a perfect match. "That's branding," I said to myself sarcastically. Beyond dismayed by how the day had gone, I really wanted nothing more than to go back home. As if to punctuate just how hopeless things were, the blisters on my feet had burst and begun to bleed.

At 4:20 Artie came and found me and asked how I was doing. I tried to figure out a diplomatic way to tell him it wouldn't work out when he said, "That's okay kid," and handed me an envelope with cash inside.

"You had to see, right?"

I drove back to Burbank, threw the brush in the dumpster, and climbed the stairs to my apartment. The wheelie clanked up every stair.

Finally, the day of Amanda's shoot arrived. The location was on a studio lot, which I felt pretty excited about. Amanda had her own trailer and I set up inside to apply her makeup. Her little dog Abby greeted me like a long lost friend. Amanda was in curlers and the hairdresser was there while I did her makeup. We all talked to each other like old friends. This felt right. But I wondered what would happen tomorrow? Back to Barney's and whatever extra work I could find? I applied Amanda's makeup expertly and soon the production assistant came to gather her for her scene. I got ready to leave but Amanda said they had another artist on set that would powder her down. I disliked the idea of sitting all alone in this tiny trailer, but then Amanda asked me if I'd mind walking Abby while she was gone.

Amanda insisted on paying me extra to walk her dog. Besides, she didn't want Abby to poop in her trailer. I grabbed Abby's leash and I started to walk her on the lot. I didn't know where to go so I headed to the perimeter of the lot where I thought I might find a patch of grass so Abby could do her business.

*Ha*, I thought to myself, *this dog doesn't need a patch of grass, she needs a department store.*

I walked Abby purposefully and confidently. I had so much on my mind and Abby seemed to sense this as she walked obediently next to me.

I wanted Abby to poop so I could be sure she wouldn't do it in Amanda's trailer. I saw grass and headed past the other trailers towards it. Suddenly, one of the doors opened and Paula Poundstone stepped outside. I recognized her. I knew better than to say anything to a celebrity on a lot so I simply smiled at her. Paula said hello to me but enthusiastically greeted the dog.

"What a cute dog," she said.

"Right," I said back, "so cute."

"Hey," said Paula Poundstone, "Are you one of those professional dog walkers?"

I looked right at Paula Poundstone and considered her question.

I had two options: one, I could pitch her on being a makeup artist, which by looking at her I could tell would go nowhere. Or, two, I could tell her I was a professional dog walker and see if it might lead somewhere.

Anywhere.

"Yes! I'm a professional dog walker," I told her. Because, I reasoned with myself, by the very definition of the word 'professional,' I was someone working in such a capacity. Amanda was paying me; I was walking Abby, so therefore at that moment I was a professional dog walker.

"So," Paula said to me, "I got a dog and he's a real asshole." We both laughed at this.

"I know the type," I said.

"How much would you charge to walk him?" she asked.

OY!

I had no idea how much a dog walker would charge. No idea whatsoever. "How big is he?" I asked. Now I was just stalling for time and trying to think like a professional dog walker.

"Well, he's a big dog. Cal's his name, and he's real strong; he likes to pull. A lot."

I threw out a number based on absolutely nothing but my immediate need to not live in my car.

"I charge $25 for a half hour walk," I said. I did some quick math in my mind. If I could get $25 for a half hour that would be $50/hour, and if I worked full time that could yield $100K a year.

"Okay," Paula Poundstone said, "When can you start?"

I was amazed and excited. I arranged to walk Paula's dog in Santa Monica a few days a week.

Paula asked me if I could do any dog training. I thought back to when I was a little girl and "trained" my dog Ginger to "sit" by giving her no less than ten thousand treats while saying "sit, sit, sit," until finally she sat. It got so bad that whenever the dog would see me she would immediately sit and then drag herself around the house after me to get treats until my mother finally told us both to knock it off.

I didn't know about the training and didn't want to commit to that in case I lost the dog-walking gig. I told Paula I would need to assess her dog first. She agreed that was a good idea. As we walked away from each other she asked me for my business card.

Note to self: make dog walking business cards!

Fenway

# Like A Dog

One of the things I absolutely love about being a pet-sitter, besides the dogs, of course, is the glorious reality of personal freedom on the job. No specific work attire is required, you don't have to dress up, wear high heels, put on makeup or be at your most presentable best at any given moment. Dogs generally don't care if you took a shower that particular morning nor do they mind if you smell a little like last night's dinner. I normally wear workout clothes on the job. Not sweatpants, as they're too hot. But stretchy material so I can move freely and keep up with all the dogs. Gym shoes are a must because of all the walking. When I bothered wearing a pedometer, some days I would clock about 10 miles. Because I don't have to worry about my clothes too much, I have saved thousands of dollars on dry-cleaning since starting Your Dog's Best Friend.

The pet sitting is always changing, while the dog walking is pretty consistent. Clients rotate in and rotate out so that as soon as I start feeling like I have a regular schedule, suddenly someone wants an extra walk or a client needs me to sleep over. Typically though, I have some flexibility in my schedule unless it's the holidays and I am slammed with multiple pet-sitting jobs along with my regular four or five dog walking clients, which I call "my daily's". Thankfully, I can generally squeeze in my own life chores, which might have to be saved for a weekend or a day off. I can pick up groceries, stop at the bank, keep doctor's appointments, and squeeze in a manicure or pedicure about once a week. The manicure or pedicure has to done at the end of the day for obvious reasons, but if I am not too pooped, it's good to get it out of the way before every other working woman shows up on Saturday and Sunday. If you're stuck at a regular 9 to 5 job, you can't call the shots with your personal time. This alone is worth the small price of picking up some poop along the way. Hanging out with the dogs is a blast, but admittedly, after a while, the novelty wears off. At the end of a long, sweaty day in the sun, I occasionally think about my friends in their designer clothes having meetings in air-conditioned offices and eating lunch with clients at fancy restaurants. And then I think, is this really better or just different?

And that leads to the flip side of all that personal freedom. I have to get up super early every morning and I am *not* a morning person and usually I end my day by lying my head down on someone else's pillow. If I am doing overnights then I have to figure out how long it will take me to get to my first client house from wherever I am staying. And when I have to check in at the next house. Packing up requires a lot of extra time. I usually wash the sheets and re-make the bed, take out the garbage, make sure the mail is all inside, pick up any dog shit from the yard, remove my food from the fridge, take my items from the shower and bathroom sink. The list goes on. Ironically, I have never created a checklist. I just do it. I have hardly ever left things behind. One time, I left yogurt and some bottled water at a client's and the client called to tell me I left it behind only to follow up with a request to book me for more overnights in a few short weeks. When I first started the business, I was booked solid for weeks straight at client houses. I never slept at home and my landlord was beginning to suspect I had moved out. I considered putting all my things into storage and house-sitting to save money but the thought of having no place to call home was a bit scary so I scrapped that idea.

I usually begin the checking out process the night before I leave a house, especially if I have been staying for a long time and have spread out. For short jobs, three days to a week, I might live out of my overnight bag especially if the job is close to my own house. It's nice to be able to run home in the morning and get ready there.

However, if a job is particularly long, I shower and get ready at the client's house and might have two or three overnight bags. I always try to leave the client's home in a slightly better condition than when I found it. This was mostly impossible in the case of a spotless home, but all I could strive for in these circumstances was to leave the house with no sign that I had been there at all.

The initial meeting for the overnight stays can be awkward. There is always that moment where I ask the client, "Where should I sleep?" And the husband and wife (usually it's a couple) look at each other, and if they don't have a guest bedroom, they have me sleep in their bed. Of course, this can make some people uncomfortable, but once they think about what's best for their dog they usually get used to the idea.

I had one man, who was quite rude; ask me if I was going to have sex in his and his wife's bed. Only he asked in a much blunter and crasser way.

This surprised me, but I imagine it's on everyone's mind. The truth is, I've slept with more dogs than people and I don't mind it one bit. Sure, they can snore and make noises and all sorts of other things, but in most cases I find dogs are good snugglers and fantastic company.

After I told this man it was $100, he said "An hour?"

I felt like reminding him I'm a pet-sitter, not a prostitute. One sleeps with you and the other sleeps with your dog.

The dogs absolutely seem grateful to have me there, and even though

I am not their "real" Mom I think there is a certain understanding on their part that I am there for them.

The majority of overnight jobs are in relatively nice homes. I have become more discerning over time and rarely sleep at my client's homes these days. I am grateful to have that part mostly hired out. My fee starts at $100 per night and sometimes a little more depending on any ancillary work I have to do in the house, such as excessive watering or personal assistant stuff. Occasionally I agree to ship mail or pay bills for a client who is going to be away for an extended amount of time.

The initial client visit is absolutely mandatory and I have always believed it should be free of charge. Some companies charge for this, but I never have. I typically arrange the first meeting at the client's convenience, so this means a night or a weekend, which is fine with me.

The worst type of pet-sitting job is when someone else will be there while the job is being done. It's hard not to feel like that person staying at the house should be doing your job. So here you are, a virtual stranger to this family, and you've been hired to look after the pets and family home while another person is staying there. That person could be there for any number of reasons. For instance, they live there but didn't go on the trip and won't be home during the day. Like a 20-something who is basically on his or her own but hasn't moved out of the house yet, so they might have a full time job but cannot squeeze a dog walk in. The worst is a relative who is staying at the house more for his or her own benefit than for the families. This particular scenario drives me nuts. Some guests are resentful that they weren't entrusted to look after the pets and they might act in a hostile way towards a paid pet-sitter. Especially if this particular person is short on cash and sees your check sitting there on the first day worth a couple hundred bucks. This person might waste a lot of your time telling you their life story or asking how much you charge or telling you about all the reasons they are staying at the house (freeloading) but not doing any of the actual work (irresponsible). The guest at a home you are working at can really screw you up, too. Leaving the door open so a cat or dog can get out, feeding the dog table scraps while you aren't there so there is crime scene diarrhea to clean up when you arrive. Reporting erroneous information back to the owner such as you never came- (they were passed out when you did) or flat out lying and claiming you never came at all and maybe the owners should cancel the check and pay them instead.

The best part about this gig by far is the dogs. I adore dogs; big ones, little ones, old ones and young ones. Dogs are like people and every one of them has to be judged on their own merits. In some cases, I feel so close to the dogs and I have developed such a bond with them, I want to call up their human's and ask to speak with the dogs. That's how much I miss them. I have gotten a bit depressed over it and of course have bawled right along with my clients when the inevitable happens. It is not typical in most jobs to have a "client" die. Especially when you have been doing this for almost fifteen years and have the absolute pleasure of their company here on this earth for such a short amount of time.

I get to know my two-legged clients reasonable well, and have become friends with some of them. Most of them maintain a professional distance, but a few have concluded since I have the keys to their house they may as well drop all pretenses and be their true selves. After all, once you've seen a client's vibrator tossed carelessly under her bed, covered in cat hair, is there anything left to hide?

Auggie

# Furry Children

*Anthropomorphism*: As defined by the modern American dictionary, is a type of personification that gives human characteristics to non-humans or objects, *especially animals.*

Especially animals! Not just animals though. No, specifically our pets. And by that I mean mainly our dogs. I can't be the only one. I tell my dog everything, including where I am going and, when I will be back. Of course, I always tell him I'll be right back, to reassure him. When I return home I always ask him how his day was. When I enter the house, Dexter always gets up and greets me, then follows me around, like a child.

People baby talk to their dogs, send them to school (for training), and buy them treats and toys, and anything else that can be dreamed up. Don't believe me? Then just check out one of those big-box pet stores on any given day.

Chances are, though, you do believe me or else you wouldn't be reading this book.

The pet product market is over 62 billion dollars and that is in the U.S. alone, according to the American Pet Product Association. But why do we spend so much money on our furry friends? Is it because furry children don't steal our credit cards and wreck our cars?

Or is it because all the money we spend on our pets validates us calling them our furry children? Or are our pets so helpless and vulnerable on top of adorably cute that we cannot help but treat them like our non-furry kids? I don't have the answers to these questions and I'm not complaining. I love all dogs. There are no good breeds and no bad breeds. There are only dogs and the people that own and shape them. Dogs, like humans, are shaped by their experiences…if a dog learns fear, that dog may become aggressive. The fear stays in the memory forever and it can manifest itself as fear aggression, or fear anxiety or general anxiety. Dogs, it turns out have the capacity to feel all the emotions humans can, and possibly even more nuanced than humans.

Sure, they might make their share of trouble, such as biting the neighbors and chewing up the furniture, but isn't it worth it once you see that adorable face? Can anyone resist the pitter-patter of little paws? Isn't it utterly addicting the way your dog greets you when you come home?

Can we in all seriousness say we're getting that same love and adoration from our human kids? I'll even give the teenage ones a pass because I'm sympathetic to "hormonal changes" at the moment.

Let's face it, pets are our family and in some cases, they are better than family. Certain members anyway. They have better manners and they are excellent listeners. When was the last time you had a conversation with your dog and you caught him sneaking glances at his cell phone? Or lying about his homework?

Karen, a woman and mother of four, who is a great client of mine and has been for years, put it like this:

"I have four kids, and out of all of them, he's the best." She was talking about her Pomeranian, Max, of course.

Many a client, but mostly the ones without "real" children, have taken it upon themselves not only to treat their pets like furry children but also to spoil them just like a human kid might become spoiled.

I had a client insist I arrive at her house at 10:30 a.m. and 3:30 p.m. everyday because her dog could not be alone for more than five hours. That was the limit she set in her mind for the maximum amount of time her dog could be alone. It did not matter that the dog was able to sleep through the night going eight or more hours without getting up. Nope, five hours alone was the maximum.

This client insisted I count out exactly thirty-five pieces of veterinarian prescribed kibble at each visit and hand feed them to her dog once they were warmed to the exact right temperature. She claimed her dog had a delicate stomach and would not tolerate eating anything other than this very specific diet hand administered at this exact temperature. I didn't have the heart to tell her I'd seen her dog eat her own poop.

After all, without these people who treat their pets like furry children, I would be out of business.

I've been a professional pet-sitter and dog walker for the past fifteen years and I have made my living taking care of other people's pets. I believe it is a valuable service and a worthwhile way to spend my time. And not because I couldn't find any other work. In fact, I have been many other things but none as satisfying or rewarding as caring for other living creatures.

I am grateful to have clients who heap gratitude and thanks on me not to mention pay me my rate. I feel satisfaction and pride when clients tell me that they couldn't do their jobs unless I did mine.

Every pet feels like my own and I treat each one like I would like someone to take care of my dog, Dexter. Dexter is MY canine soul mate, so I absolutely get it when a client says they worry about their dog or they want what is best for their dog.

Though I am a pet-sitter, the majority of my clients are dog owners. The name of my business is, Your Dog's Best Friend and I take that name very seriously. I have also taken care of cats, bunnies, birds, reptiles, fish, llamas, and even a Vietnamese potbelly pig once. I went vegan after that and couldn't even look at bacon let alone smell it.

People have fallen in love with being in love with their dogs. I have seen dogs eat furniture, destroy valuables, and wreck havoc on relationships.

I once had newlyweds as clients. The woman had her dog before she got married and the dog managed to outlast the husband. Part of the problem, from what I observed, was that the husband always referred to the dog, named Cali, as "it."

"Honey, the dog walker is here to walk it."

"Darling, I've told you a million times the dog is a her. The dog walker is here to walk *her.*"

Which escalated to, "Goddamnit! I told you a million times the dog is a she, a girl, feminine, not an it. Why can't you comprehend that?"

And then, the mail arrived from the divorce attorneys.

The dog can do no wrong. The dog is an unending supply of unconditional love. Even if he has just eaten a hole in the door to the backyard the same size as his head or peed on the priceless Persian rug.

The last 15 years has been a whirlwind of incredible experiences involving people's pets and homes. I have been honored to take care of and know so many wonderful creatures and their human-counterparts.

I've taken care of celebrity dogs with enviable wardrobes that have travelled in the lap of luxury to every continent. I've cared for the young and old and sick and healthy alike. And I've fallen in love with all of them a little bit. So I totally understand the love between a pet and its owner (and I hate that word but it is the most direct and legally correct).

A woman called me recently very concerned, and the tone of her voice told me she was upset about something. She told me she was going back into the work force after spending the last ten years at home to raise her three kids. They ranged in ages from 9 to 15. Her real worry was her 6 year-old Maltese who was "like a daughter to her" and she was not sure how well the dog would handle it when she too was suddenly gone all day. I told her about the dog walking and pet-sitting visits I offered, but she asked me if I would consider offering doggie day care for her dog. In all honesty, I would have loved to have another client but in good conscience I could not promise her doggie day care when I was in and out of my house most days like it was a revolving door and her dog would probably be better off at home.

We discussed her dog's personality. "Does your dog like other dogs?" I asked. "Well no," she said. She then went on to describe her dog the identical way she might describe one of her kids. "Chloe is an introverted-extrovert. She won't make the first move to play with someone, but if they make a friendly overture towards her then she'll probably want to play."

"Friendly overture?" This was a dog we were talking about.

Finally, I said to this woman, "I think your dog will be okay at home by herself. Maybe she might even like a little down time." The dog was only going to be alone for a few hours in the morning before the kids filled up the house again. "Besides," I said, "don't you have a lot on your plate to think about?"

I can't even imagine the stress of re-entering the workforce after ten years as a stay at home mom. I'm having anxiety just thinking about it.

"I know," she said, "but she's the baby." This woman was practically in tears. Now maybe, just maybe, she was transferring all the anxiety she felt about a new job or worries over her actual human children onto the dog, but somehow I doubt it. Our animals depend on us so completely that we practically lose our minds arranging for them to have their needs met.

One of those needs is medical, of course, and I could fill an entire other book with all the medical issues I have helped my clients address with their pets.

Zeus, a sweet terrier takes a Pepcid every night before bedtime for his acid-reflux. The dog has acid reflux! Sure, they managed in the wild for thirty thousand years and now that they're domesticated they need reflux medicine. Another client with a miniature pinscher has me give his dog Viagra every night. And not for what you might think. Before Viagra was what it is today, it was a heart medicine and so the dog takes it for his heart.

There is nothing quite as tender as the love we have for our beloved children, and the same proves true for the furry kind, especially when no human kids are involved.

When no human children are involved, it is impossible to have any reference point for what it's like to have real, live human children. I might not put my life on the line for my dog, even though I love him to death, but I would definitely do so for my kids.

A lovely older couple I've worked with for years recently had me stay at their home with their aging dogs because one of them had to go into the hospital. The entire situation was rife with tension and concern. Not just for one another, but for the pets, too.

"How many days is it between Tuesday and Friday?"

I attempted to answer diplomatically.

Suzanne and Richard really started to go at it. Suzanne was always the softest spoken, until she wasn't.

"Richard," Suzanne said, trying to control her rising voice, "if you go into the hospital on Tuesday and you come out on Friday, you've only been in the hospital three days, because you don't count the fourth day. You're getting out that day."

"Yes dear, I understand, but you see, if I come out on Friday I'll have spent the whole day there, so that will count as four days."

They were having an argument in response to the simple question I had posed, "How many nights will you need me to sleep over?"

They were both right. Kind of. And suddenly I understood it was not only the days but also the nights, and these two were probably scared shitless to spend any time away from each other or their girls.

They had no kids. Only dogs. Dogs that they bred and showed and loved and displayed their ribbons and trophies and pictures.

The dogs were gorgeous, too. Goldens. Mostly girls, and one boy who had passed and his remains were on the mantle near a picture-perfect finish of his crossing some finishing line to win a large silver trophy.

They were looking to me to sleep over in their home while Suzanne slept in the hospital with Richard. She had already arranged this with Richard's doctor while Richard underwent a back procedure. It was being done in some upscale surgery center and Suzanne could stay right by his side. I felt sorry for Richard. I'm sure he could have used a tiny break from Suzanne. They had been together since high school. Love at first sight. I heard the story. See, when you're a pet-sitter, you are so much more than someone who just comes in and takes care of pets. You are a confidant and friend, sounding board and therapist, shoulder to cry on, and person to be relied upon. Many of my clients have become my friends.

I walked their girls everyday, twice a day, even though it was a royal pain in the butt to navigate traffic to where they lived near the Beverly Center from where I lived in the San Fernando Valley. But I did it because they wouldn't take another walker. They loved me, I assured them they would love the other walker but they wouldn't hear of it.

Suzanne worked part-time for a doctor at UCLA. She was very bright and well educated. Richard owned his own manufacturing plant and had messed up his back lifting something at work.

They wanted me to sleep with their dogs and help them onto the bed. The girls weighed about 85lbs each, and they were old girls too. Sarah and Rose-Marie were their names. They were beauties. They never had a cross word or cross growl between them, except over food. They had cushiony pet stairs leading up to the bed on either side so the girls could climb up and sleep with them in bed or get on the bed whenever they wanted. Some people have a strict no dogs in the bedroom policy, but I have no clients like that. I looked at their bed. It looked like a bed an old couple had slept in for the last decade along with a brood of various dogs the weight of small children.

The girls wagged their tails at me while I spoke to Suzanne and Richard. Both of them had long hair, red, shiny and smooth. They were gorgeous and so smiley I wanted to hug them. I could see why Richard and Suzanne loved them so much.

I tried to ease Suzanne's worry about them, while silently

acknowledging Richard's procedure and how she needed to be present for him. Every surface in this entire house was filled with mementos of their life at dog shows, plus their wedding picture. A gorgeous black and white wedding picture in an 8 X10 frame of the two of them when they were much younger. Suzanne with her tiny figure in a tailored ivory gown and Richard in a tux, pressed close cheek to cheek.

Suzanne was happy to hold every precious picture in her hand and relive all the memories of their dogs. I was happy to hear her stories. I wanted to make certain she understood that I really do get it when people tell me their dogs are their furry children.

Richard had his procedure and all went well. The girls behaved themselves. I slept in their bed, feeling their girls at my feet. I walked and fed them, and assured them their parents would be back soon. I could tell they were moping around a bit. I gave them lots of love, and when Suzanne and Richard's car finally pulled into the driveway to drop them off, I said to the girls, "Mommy and Daddy are home!" And unlike the non-furry kids, who might not be able to pull themselves away from a screen or a phone, the girls were way ahead of me, wagging their tails and waiting at the door.

Barkley

# Dog Walkers

The primary consternation of any employer's existence is its employees. It doesn't matter if you have one employee or a thousand; there is always going to be the same issues and challenges. Absenteeism, tardiness and stealing are just to name a few. Large companies have human resource departments to handle these issues as well as procedures in place for hiring and training new employees. As a sole proprietor of a small business, all of these tasks fall in your lap along with a heap of others.

Admittedly, I am not the type of person who relinquishes control well, but don't consider myself a control freak, per se. You could surmise that I don't very much care for being at the mercy of other people's reliability.

When it's my phone blowing up because a dog walker didn't show up or the dog has gone missing, the buck stops with me. I am the boss and I have to put up or shut up; solve my customer's problems or potentially lose their business.

Let's be real here, this is dog walking and pet sitting, it's not brain surgery or rocket science. My philosophy has always been to tell people what to do, not how to do it. And then to give them a ton of leeway as to *when* to do it. I always allow dog walkers flexibility in their daily schedules. All my clients know that the time we arrive to look after their pets is a time range. We cannot promise to be anywhere exactly on time everyday, this is Los Angeles after all and traffic is about as unpredictable as a stray dog. I bring dog walkers with me to meet the client and the dog before we actually start providing our service. I don't offer on-demand dog walking. No one is showing up somewhere I have never been myself, that's just good business and for the safety of everyone. I would not ask any of my dog walkers to do anything I wouldn't do myself. I have always considered anyone I've hired to be part of the team and expressed to them my gratitude and how much I appreciate their work. I have been blessed to have hired and still to this day, have on my team, some of the most amazing people and I am extremely thankful for them. Because honestly, relying on other people to represent you or your business is not for the faint of heart.

One might think that dog walking and pet sitting is relatively simple if they had no prior knowledge of it. But in fact, where furry children and people's homes are involved, it can get complicated. What should be relatively straightforward can become a nightmare if everything doesn't go according to plan. Alarms are set off, people get locked out, people get locked in. Once I got locked in somewhere myself.

I have learned that I should never assume that anyone has the same common sense that I have; I'm looking at you, the walker that threw out dog poop in my client's kitchen trash! More than once…

While I strive to avoid problems, dogs get away, cats never come back, the pool floods, the neighbor's dog bites you, your car gets a flat, shit happens. And that's okay, it's not that shit happens, it's how you clean up afterwards that counts. The only thing I ever asked of anyone on the team is to keep in touch with *me*. Keep the lines of communication open with me. That's all, the number one rule.

I don't write this with any intentional malice or to assassinate any one person's character. I believe people are all inherently good, we all have

Buddha nature. It's my opinion that everyone is doing the best they can, given the circumstances they are working with. Obviously there are exceptions to this rule. But for the purposes of this book, I am simply trying to convey the frustrations and betrayals I experienced all while trying to hire reliable and dependable dog walkers and pet sitters. These experiences represent a composite collection of my most baffling episodes with other people. To be clear, I am fictionalizing true stories.

When Your Dog's Best Friend became marginally successful (meaning, I was paying my bills and had a little savings) I found myself walking more dogs than I could handle. I decided to hire other dog walkers.

I was reluctant to take this leap for a few reasons. One, because I was only just starting to make any money and I didn't want to share it, and two, because most of my clients loved me and trusted me and I wasn't sure about handing over the reins to potentially unknown commodities. "Outsourcing is business 101," a friend of mine with an MBA told me. "Work on your business not in your business" was popular advice thanks to the great book, *The E-Myth* written by Michael E. Gerber.

Hiring is the key to growing any small business, and so reluctantly I reached out to find dog walkers to take some clients off my hands, so I could concentrate on growing the business and work on marketing. At one point I even fantasized about ringing the bell on the New York Stock Exchange for the opening day of trading for YDBF. I really thought the business model had potential and at the time no one was dog walking professionally, I didn't know it then, but I was pioneering the dog walking industry.

Prior to the creation of the pet care service industry, most dog walkers were friends, friends of friends or neighbor's kids who flaked at the first better offer. I really feel I shaped the dog walking industry and lead the way for future trailblazers. Unfortunately or fortunately, however you want to look at it, hiring other dog walkers became the undoing of the business. You see, while some dog walkers went on to become great friends, others turned out to be well, assholes. Looking back, some of the situations are funny but mostly they were horrible, embarrassing, downright frustrating, and occasionally dangerous. But most of all, hiring dog walkers was disheartening at times and cost me some of my best clients. I'm talking my A-list clients like Dr. Dre.

Initially, I turned to *Craigslist* to hire dog walkers. This is after I exhausted asking all my friends and family. Oh and by the way, never hire your friends or family as they have the potential to harm your business even more than a stranger.

I ran my first ad on *Craigslist* and listed my toll-free number. I didn't want to see resumes, I wanted people to call and talk with me so I could gauge their excitement about walking dogs. I wanted to hire people who loved dogs as much as me and would just be happy to spend time in the great outdoors with man's best friend.

Here's what I got instead; a lot of people who wanted to know how much the job pays. That's the first question I'd say about fifty percent of the people who called would ask. That information was in the ad. Say what you want about *Craigslist* being a train wreck and all that but they do allow you to write a very comprehensive advertisement for basically anything you want.

As someone who has worked in recruiting and staffing I can absolutely tell you that unless you're applying to be a hit man, don't ask how much the job pays as your first question about the position. And the second thing is, don't have another person call on your behalf. I had countless moms and dads and even husbands and wives call on behalf of another person, for the job. I can guarantee you, if you don't have the motivation or energy to make the call yourself, you probably won't get the job. No matter how much of a go-getter your mom tells me you are.

So there I was, taking call after call and eliminating most of the people simply by the sound of their voice and their words. Don't speak English; don't like dogs, live too far away, under age, just got out of prison, etc.

I hate hiring people. People always tell you what they know you want to hear. Once, I inadvertently hired a crack whore. The woman told me she had been on drugs in the past and she was clean now and that I should give her a chance. I wanted to help her. She said something to me that resounded with me and so I thought I could trust her. What she said to me was very earnest, probably something a liar wouldn't say.

She said to me, during the interview, that she was, "a good number two." She told me she wasn't capable of being the boss, she knew that about herself. But she thought she took direction quite well, and if she could just have one more chance, she wouldn't fuck up. I believed her. I looked at her hands while she was speaking. She had black letters tattooed on all her fingers. I couldn't tell what it spelled out. Her name was Molly and she had a young son. I felt sorry for her. I gave her a couple clients in Sherman Oaks. She lived in Valley Village, which is pretty close. On her second day of work, my client called to tell me Molly had shown up at her house with a black eye. "A black guy?" I asked my client. No, no a "black eye." When I asked Molly about it, she told me she was back with her pimp. Funny, she never mentioned a pimp when I interviewed her and asked her specifically, "Is there any reason I shouldn't give you this job?" I had to let her go after that, and the client canceled the dog walking service.

Again, I spoke to a woman who sounded good on the phone and we scheduled a time to meet at a local Starbucks.

She sounded okay, but not great, however she said the right things; she loved dogs and she was reliable. She mostly worked her own hours as a painter and did that at nights. Her days were free, she liked dogs, and she had reliable transportation. We met for coffee and she turned up on time. Great. Now, no one is expected to wear a suit and tie to a dog walking job interview but this woman took it to the next level. She was wearing denim shorts and a tube top. We sat down and spoke and she told me pretty bluntly that she wasn't a people person. I find most people will tell you the truth about themselves, if you just listen. But sometimes, and I am very guilty of this, we don't listen. We hear what we want to hear.

I wound up hiring Kelly and she worked out pretty good. I introduced her to my clients who all had the same reaction, which was "Well, if you think she's okay then she must be okay." Kelly just had to walk the dogs and leave a note for the customer at the end of the walk to say if the dog had a nice walk, and if it pooped while outside. I told Kelly not to sweat the notes too much; she didn't have to leave a novel or anything. One day, when Kelly was absent, I walked her dogs only to find the stack of notes she had been leaving for the clients went something like this; *Me walk dog, dog take shit.* I could not believe the crudeness of her notes and the graphic detail in which she would describe the dog's bowel movements. After that incident, I purchased preprinted report cards, which she could check off as an alternative.

Now, in this current age of technology, we text clients from our smart phones and include pictures from the walk so notes aren't necessary. I do know clients, however, who saved the notes from their dog walkers and included them in their memory books.

Kelly eventually went on to bigger and better things but not before creating a situation for me in which there was no winning. I had arranged for her to sleepover at a clients house in Bel-Air. Their house was decked out in the nicest of everything, including a family room with expensive, imported rugs. On the last day of the job, while the clients were en route home, one of the dogs pooped on the heirloom rug. I don't know why the dog pooped on the rug, he just did. I don't mean to imply Kelly wasn't letting the dog out or doing her job, because dogs do poop on rugs sometimes, even if they've had a chance to go outside.

When the clients arrived home, they walked in on Kelly sitting in their family room, watching their flat screen television, and sampling their gourmet popcorn while a pile of dog poop "dried" on their carpet. Needless to say, the client called me to complain and I had to go over there. Kelly was very calm about the whole thing and explained that by letting the poop dry up it would be easier to remove from the carpet.

The client was livid and insisted Kelly should have picked up the poop right away and spot treated the rug. I had no choice but to side with the client even though I have to admit Kelly presented a good argument. I paid for the entire rug to be cleaned, which cost me more than the whole job was worth. Of course, I still paid Kelly too, so the job was a loser. I had a long talk with Kelly after that about customers NOT coming home to find dog shit on their rugs or anywhere else.

The worst dog walker I ever hired was a woman I'm going to call Calamity. Calamity was on the heavier side but she told me she hoped to lose weight by dog walking, and maybe even get healthier and happier because of the time she would spend with the dogs.

I felt sorry for Calamity, I know what a struggle it is to lose weight and I really wanted to see her become a healthier person. Some dog walkers clock five or even ten miles a day on their pedometers so if you couple that with watching what you eat, you will lose weight.

Calamity had a nice enough personality but often screwed up and then apologized so profusely I would always give her another chance. One could say Calamity was passive-aggressive. It seemed to me she was sabotaging my business and when I confronted her about it she didn't deny it, but didn't exactly confirm it, either.

For starters, I had this wonderful client who lived in a two-story house. She had a gorgeous German Shepard who needed to go for a walk everyday because the client worked long hours in the music business. One day, Calamity went over to her house as scheduled, only she didn't take the dog for a walk or even let the dog out. Instead, she helped herself to the contents of the client's fridge and made herself a sandwich. After she ate the sandwich, Calamity used the bathroom for a long time and then left, but not before leaving the client a lovely note about how great her dog had been on the walk.

I know all this because the client called me from upstairs as she had been working from home that day and knew exactly what had happened. The client was furious, she yelled at me for a long time and held nothing back. She never wanted to see Calamity again and I was fired and the company was fired.

I apologized the entire time; I could not believe Calamity would do such a thing. I had to fix it so I asked the customer what would make it better. Ultimately I had to go and walk the dog myself for free, of course, for I don't remember how long it took to get back in her good graces.

I called Calamity and asked her if all this was true and she admitted it. She had gone to the clients, made a sandwich, used the bathroom and left without even letting the dog out, for goodness sake. He had a backyard!

Calamity was embarrassed and claimed she had IBS and her stomach had been hurting and she needed to eat something, but then she needed the bathroom and that took a long time, so she didn't have any time left to walk the dog. I felt compassion for Calamity. I felt sorry for the dog too, prancing around in the kitchen, watching *his* dog walker make a sandwich, waiting for the walk and not getting to go outside to relieve himself. I didn't fire Calamity because she begged me to give her "one more chance."

I gave her another chance and a chance after that. I had another client who wanted her dog walked at noon. The client unexpectedly came home from work at 10:30 a.m. one day only to see the note from this particular dog walker saying the dog had a nice walk at noon and it wasn't even noon yet. The client called me super pissed off. Again I called Calamity and she gave me a story of having a doctor's appointment and she had to walk the dog early.

The resolution was that Calamity had to call the client when she was at her house so the client could be sure she was doing her job-at the right time. Ultimately, I had to let Calamity go when she cost me one of my best clients.

This client lived in Malibu and had a ton of people that worked for her, in her home. The dog, Brandy, was well behaved and had travelled all over the world. An ideal situation, an easy to care for dog and an amazing house. This client was rarely home, paid on time, and left generous tips and gifts, especially around the holidays. I would have managed the client myself if I hadn't lived so far away and so I counted on Calamity. Calamity had even received an expensive spa treatment gift on her birthday, which is why I don't comprehend why Calamity would screw her (and me) over so badly.

The client was going out of town for the holidays and wanted Calamity to sleep over and to sleep in her master bedroom (overlooking the ocean) with the dog. This bedroom was bigger than Calamity's entire apartment. And, she had permission to use the entire house-pool, spa, chef's kitchen, everything. It was understood that the housekeeper would be staying at the house continuing to do her duties. The housekeeper had her own quarters at the house. The dog was an older Rhodesian ridgeback and knew Calamity well. On the second day of the job, the client called me, absolutely livid from Switzerland. Apparently, Calamity decided that the bed, which was a Cali-King, was not comfortable enough with the dog in it and she had thrown the dog out in the night.

The housekeeper had been woken up by the dog crying trying to get back into the master bedroom, and had asked Calamity why she wasn't allowing the dog to sleep with her. Calamity told her she didn't want the dog in bed with her. This lady was paying top dollar so her dog could sleep in the master bedroom with Calamity and Calamity flat out refused.

The client was upset and told me she felt betrayed, she told me what a piece of shit Calamity is and how could she betray her dog like this not to mention her. I offered to go and sleep at her house myself, which she refused. Instead, she fired Calamity and me but not before adding that she had never met a fat dog walker in her life and she doubted Calamity had even been walking her dog because Calamity had only gotten heavier. Which was true.

I called Calamity immediately and fired her. She wasn't even upset. I asked her if she was trying to lose me all my clients because she had successfully done that. She pretty much admitted she was starting her own dog care business and was in fact trying to lose me my clients. She asked me if I would write her a letter of recommendation, which I refused. Once I was able to compose myself, which took some time, I calmly explained to her what a terrible employee she was and how much damage she had done to my business when I had been only trying to help her.

A few weeks passed and I received a letter of apology from Calamity saying she had reflected on her transgressions and that she took responsibility and was very sorry for everything she had done. While I did appreciate the apology it was a little too late for that. If anything, this was a valuable lesson to me about not giving someone too many chances.

In my defense, good help (or really, any help for that matter) is hard to find. I would have walked all these dogs myself if you could line them all up tail-to-tail but my clients were spread out across Los Angeles and the valley so it was not physically possible.

While all these shenanigans were going on with the dog walkers I was teaching a class on pet sitting and dog walking and recall being asked what the biggest threat to me personally was while doing this job. I remember saying, "The dog walkers, the people you hire will drive you to an early grave if you're not careful- or they could even cost you your business. That's the biggest threat."

In the fifteen plus years I have spent working as an entrepreneur running a professional dog walking and pet sitting company, I have encountered almost every type of betrayal by an employee. Except thank goodness, with the exception of stealing clients, no one has ever stolen anything from a client.

When I hire employees I tell them there is a nanny-cam in every single room of every single house and I caution them not to do anything they wouldn't want to see themselves doing on Court TV.

The ultimate and most unexpected betrayal came from a young woman I hired named Joy. It is pretty ironic her name was Joy because she caused the exact opposite. Joy came to me with a new degree from an Ivy League University and an eagerness to work side by side with me and manage the business. I cannot recall how I came to meet her, however I do remember that I was thrilled with this young capable woman with her shiny ideas and degree. I spoke with her at length and decided she would learn all the ins and outs of the business and manage the customers and other dog walkers, and she would earn a percentage of the business. I was thrilled to have this dog-walker, manager, and consultant, with her new degree come and work with me. I thought we made an excellent team and I was looking forward to her applying her business acumen to my dog-walking business.

I was so happy to have someone so bright and enthusiastic working for Your Dog's Best Friend that I booked a vacation to Hawaii as I had not been anywhere for at least ten years.

I spent countless hours with Joy walking up and down the hilly streets of Santa Monica and Brentwood, Malibu, and the Pacific Palisades. I introduced her to all the clients as my new manager, I felt so proud of her. She was by all outwardly appearances a delightful human being and I enjoyed her company. We spent many a day together walking dogs and bonding. We discussed everything under the stars from dogs to philosophy and back again. At the time I was beginning to think about an idea I had for an invention. The idea had come to me while I was dog walking, that there should be wipes on the dog poop bags. I shared this idea with Joy but never even asked her to sign an NDA. (An NDA is a non-disclosure agreement, which is a legal document.) I mentioned to her that I was having people sign NDA's when I told them about my invention and she told me no worries as she had an invention she was working on as well and she would share it with me as a way of reciprocation.

We were walking along Rockingham, which is just off of Sunset Blvd. where I had about a dozen A-list clients. We were each walking two German shepherds. The German shepherds were from the home of a famous couple that were extremely successful and wealthy. They had private planes, multiple houses, and so on. I had only met with them briefly but interacted mostly with the estate manager. That's how it is with certain clients. They hire estate managers or assistants and they discuss the dog schedules and care with you. In most cases you might not even meet the actual human clients, which is fine by me as you are really just there for the dogs.

Joy and I were walking and it was a beautiful spring day. My feelings towards Joy were that of friendship and mentorship, I believed we were enjoying each other's company, and that there was a mutual respect between the two of us. As we were walking the dogs Joy began to tell me the saddest story I had ever heard.

One of Joy's distant relatives back east had married a young woman and they had a baby together. It turns out the young woman was an attorney and planning to return to work early for an important meeting regarding the firm giving her a high profile case.

As Joy explained it, this woman was a real go-getter and was not particularly liked by the husband's family as she seemed a bit too ambitious, especially as she wanted to return to her power job so shortly after having her baby girl, Sarah. The day care center this woman was going to have watch Sarah was not open as early as she needed to get to work on this particular morning.

The father-in-law offered to take the baby to the day care center on his way to work. On the morning of, the father-in-law was running late and the young woman was upset and they exchanged angry words. The woman loaded the sleeping baby in her car seat in the father-in-laws vehicle and they both left. The father-in-law was meant to drop Sarah at day care while the young attorney would get her big case, which would help make her a partner in the firm one-day.

Only none of that happened because the father-in-law was so upset by the argument that he got on the freeway and went to work forgetting to drop the baby at the day care center. Sadly, the baby died in her car seat leaving the entire family completely devastated.

At the end of this complete bummer of a story which had me crying, Joy told me her invention was a car seat alarm, which goes off if you turn off the car and the baby seat is not moved. I admired this idea and we had a lengthy discussion on inventions and patents, motherhood, and what it meant to be a working woman. So, we really bonded and I emphasize this because what happened next is completely unfathomable. I bet you think she steals my idea for the invention, right? Wrong.

I had just arrived in Hawaii and turned my phone on to eighteen new messages. I'm not that popular so I immediately know shit must be going down.

I listened to message after message from various clients letting me know that Joy had approached them to offer her own services, and she'd like to get them on board by offering them new client specials, slightly below my prices. Most of my clients were confused and a few were even amused. Some of them even hired her. To my utter satisfaction, though, one of my clients threw her out of his house.

I had one particularly uncomfortable conversation with the Rockingham Estate manager who was British and who had worked for these people for many years and had seen it all. "Look," she said to me. "Really, you can't trust anyone…she's offering better pricing." "Okay," I said, "I will match her pricing." "No," she told me, "she's here and you're not and we're going with her." I looked at my phone and started crying. The feeling of betrayal was giving me a visceral reaction that I can still conjure up even after all this time.

I called Joy because I was confused and incredulous with disbelief and to her credit this bitch, this absolute Judas answered the phone. And not only does she answer her phone but she answers in a sing-songy way with the name of her new company, which was something like, "Your Dog's Turd Wrangler."

"Joy," I said, "what's going on?" She explained to me, like I'm an idiot, that she was starting her own dog walking business.

Joy told me how swell she thought I was but that I had failed to have her sign a non-compete so she could help herself to my business and clients. She told me she admired me and even added that I am, "really pretty" (that asshole!) and that she was having a hard time getting even *one* of my clients to jump ship, but she was working on it and to please not be upset because she was only doing it because she respected me. I asked Joy if she took ANY ethics classes at her Ivy League University because if she had she would know that what she is doing is unethical. She told me not to be bitter and I should be flattered because she thought highly of me and that I had a very good business model.

I was standing at the carousel watching my lonely bag go around and around, feeling completely crushed by this betrayal. I considered grabbing my bag and getting on the next flight back to L.A., finding Joy, and punching her in the face. I am beyond pissed off and so I called Joy again and told her she is an unethical backstabber and she told me she wouldn't tolerate name-calling and hung up. I called Joy back no less than a dozen times, each time leaving her messages about what an awful person she is and how karma will get her and if karma doesn't get her I certainly would.

I got to my hotel, which of course, is not as wonderful as I'd hoped, and under construction. I found the business center and sent Joy a scathing e-mail with my solid sound bytes and then I had to call my customers. The tricky part is that I had handed over everything to Joy. All my clients' keys, alarm codes, cell phone numbers, and my endorsement of Joy. Everything. I had basically given her the keys to the castle, and she couldn't have planned her coup at a better time because she was *supposed* to be there, walking these client's dogs, and had my permission and blessing, which I had given her, never once considering this would happen.

On top of everything else, this was an embarrassing situation for me. Embarrassing is an understatement. Embarrassing is when you tuck your skirt into your panties and stroll around the mall. Embarrassing is stepping in dog shit and walking around someone's carpeted house, embarrassing is calling a client by their dog's name. I've done all these things and still managed to live.

This was beyond embarrassing, I was mortified.

I had only been singing this woman's praises to my clients in the last weeks and then the next week begging them not to move forward with her. In my entire life I never thought I'd be capable of murdering someone, until then.

My trip sucked. I sulked on the beach, drank too much, and fantasized about the slow ways I could make this woman suffer. Oh, and one more thing. That was my honeymoon.

In the end only a few of my clients went with her but they were good ones. All clients are good ones! I was so hurt by this betrayal. I went over all our conversations again and again in my head to see where I might have missed seeing this coming. I spent hours in my car driving around and picking up dogs and dropping off dogs, mentally masturbating about how I would even the score with her. I even began to stalk her at my former client's homes. I fantasized about walking my dog Dexter near to where I knew she would be walking this super-aggressive Cujo dog and hope that he would at least yank her arm out of her socket- without harming Dexter, of course.

I wanted to demonstrate to the clients that had deserted me that Joy was inept and unethical. I thought about getting back at her for hours on end. I would drive places and look for her Lexus. I would think about her dying and how much I would enjoy watching her suffer. And finally, gratefully, I thought about it less and then less, and then never at all, but until that time, I stopped hiring people altogether and went back to walking all the dogs myself. I also focused on my invention, moving forward a little bit everyday until eventually; I got it to market.

During the long process of getting my product on the shelves, I joined invention groups, attended meet-ups for patent-seekers, and spoke to hundreds of would-be inventors. Everywhere I went I made sure to share Joy's baby seat alarm idea.

Ultimately, I learned Joy moved to Florida and got married. Right before she moved she told her clients to give me a call if they still wanted dog walking. Oh yeah, this girl had nerve!

One of the couples that had been my clients, which she stole, actually reached back out to me. I went to their house. They told me that they were happy to see me and told me that they thought Joy was a wonderful person. Apparently, they never knew or claimed not to know the circumstances in which she came to walk their dogs. I told them that she was an unethical person and had basically started her business by stealing mine. They didn't care; they just wanted someone to walk their dogs.

I never saw Joy after I returned from Hawaii. Unfortunately, I've had this experience again, just not to this extreme. It never fails to amaze me when dog walkers want to up and try to steal the business. I have made it perfectly clear to so many of them that there is plenty of business to go around. I will help you if you want to start your own dog walking business and in fact, I am happy to! Just don't start your own business by stealing mine.

Many clients over the years have stayed with me through thick and thin. However, most clients come and go, especially in this business. To his credit one of my nicest clients is an attorney who had not only one but *two* different dog walkers try and steal his business and he told them both "No," and gave them a lesson on loyalty by talking their ears off for a long time about the difference between things you learn in the classroom and things you learn in life.

My experience with Joy left me with my guard up around any new person that I hired. Unfortunately, this didn't prevent me from almost coming to blows with a dog walker in a PetSmart parking lot. This was a woman I had hired who had been in the military. I assumed that if she could make it with the U.S. Government she could definitely make it as a dog walker and pet sitter, right? Wrong. I don't remember what part of the service she was in only she had been stationed in Afghanistan.

I was always a bit suspicious of this woman and wondered about her sanity. Unfortunately, I had to hire her because I really needed someone to walk a dog in Calabasas for me, in a gated community, while I was walking another client's dog in a different part of town. Honestly, it could have gone either way with this woman. I really wanted it to work out, she had been in the military and I respected that. I thought that her military experience meant she had good character and I was mistaken.

The client that lived in the gated community was an exceptional client but also a bit kooky so I was betting that the two of them would hit it off. On the very first day that Tanya (GI Jane) was supposed to walk the dog, Bo, she arrived late.

I was out of my mind with frustration! How could she be late on the first day of work? Sure, she's not working in an office environment, but it's still a paying job and someone is counting on you to be there. Tanya was supposed to arrive between 9:00 and 9:30 every morning, Monday through Friday. On Monday, her first day, the guard gate called up to the client's house to let kooky client know the dog walker was on her way up, she had checked in at the guard gate. The clients lived in the hills, on the very top of the hill. At 9:30 the dog walker still hadn't showed up at the clients.

So, to recap, the guard gate clocked her in only she never made it to the client's house. Of course at 9:30 on the dot, the client called and texted me, "Where is the dog walker?" Where, indeed. All this gives me anxiety. I am on the other side of town, walking dogs myself and of course, Tanya's phone goes right to voice mail. Perfect. Did something happen to Tanya? Did she get kidnapped? Fall into a sinkhole, abducted by strangers? I was trying to make sense of it.

I knew she knew where the client lived. I make sure to personally introduce the walkers to the clients, in the client's home. But, unbeknownst to me, the dog walking job conflicted with Tanya's yoga class, and Tanya can't do her yoga anymore so to make sure she's still getting her exercise, she decided to ride her bike to the client's house but she couldn't get her ass up the hill on her bike. Unbelievable.

Tanya finally answered her phone completely out of breath to tell me she was very sorry but she just…can't…get…up…the…hill. I remained calm and told her she needs to drive her car to the clients and consider that walking the dog was a replacement for her yoga class. So, that day the client didn't get a dog walk and I didn't get paid.

The next day, Tanya drove up to the clients but brought a menacing looking boyfriend along who hung out while Tanya was walking the dog. This made my client feel uncomfortable. I had a talk with Tanya and we went over some basics. Maybe I didn't explain them when I initially hired her. Patiently, I explained some ground rules. Rule one; drive your car there. Rule two; don't bring any boyfriends, friends, family members or ex-marines along for the ride. On day three Tanya called in sick. Apparently, riding up the hill on Monday, or attempting to, had exhausted her and now she was feverish, maybe coming down with something. On day four, Tanya showed up and told the client she was abusing drugs and alcohol and having an affair with a married man. She laid this all on my client who had just given birth and was nursing her baby and only hoped her dog could get a walk. That was the service she was paying for and entitled to. She had been my client for many years and up until this point, all the walkers had been satisfactory.

On day five, Tanya called in sick again and when I told my client, she said, "We need to go in a different direction."

Now when this happens and it does happen, people screw up, the client loses faith in my judgment, this is natural and of course, I don't like it. On top of everything else now I needed to find another person to walk this dog or the other dog and it was a big clusterfuck. This reflects poorly on me and I have the added pressure of trying to arrange walking two dogs on the opposite ends of town at the same time while trying to hire another dog walker.

Client relations are very important in this business, as with any other. However, when you supply a service such as dog walking, and are responsible for someone else's furry children, there is more at stake. Additionally, I didn't want to lose this client or any other and the dog walker had certainly not helped my client relationship.

I called Tanya and told her it wasn't going to work and she flipped out completely. She was really trying; she is doing her best, etc. She demanded that I pay her immediately the $12.50 I owed her for the one walk she actually managed to complete.

Reluctantly, I agreed to meet her at a strip mall on Ventura Boulevard and Topanga Canyon, in front of a pet store. I was only doing this out of kindness for Tanya. She said she needed the money, so I abided.

It was raining, I was exhausted, and this woman and her $12.50 were the only thing between me and getting into a nice hot bath, once I fought the traffic home. I was literally pulling into a parking place when my client called to tell me that Tanya had called her no less than fifty times begging her to give her another chance. I was livid.

I cannot believe this twat would call my client and ask for another opportunity when clearly my client wanted nothing to do with her. I pulled up and took the $12.50 from my wallet.

Tanya was standing near the entrance of the pet store while next-door there are a few construction workers working on a chain store that is going in where a Blockbuster used to be. I got out of my car and said, "Hey Tanya, don't call my client anymore, you're harassing her." Tanya responded in a very hostile manner that she could do whatever she damn well pleased. "Okay," I replied as calmly as possible, given the circumstances, then, "If you can't agree to my request then I'm not going to pay you your $12.50." Tanya instantly transformed into Tanya the terrible and goes on the attack, calling *me* names, and wanting to rip *me* a new one for not paying her and she will call whomever she fucking wants to.

I was shaking mad. I go out of my way to bring this woman $12.50, in the rain and she is standing here threatening to kick my ass. I'm suddenly beginning to see why she didn't make it in the military. I wish I had never hired her. My heart was beating like a hummingbird's, and my fight or flight response was kicking in.

Normally, I am the least confrontational person EVER and here was this evil woman wrecking havoc with my business and clients and demanding $12.50 from me.

Tanya is stunned I won't pay her because in return she won't agree to stop harassing my client and we start to yell at each other. The construction workers are beginning to chant "fight, fight" and it looked like ole miss Tanya had them on her side. It was pouring now, my kid's Christmas presents were stashed in the backseat of my car and all I could think was, *I'm going to go to jail.* I completely saw red; this is not going to end well. I was standing there yelling at this woman about $12.50, and she was saying something about the labor board and the better business bureau and I told her it would be a cold day in hell before she got the $12.50 from me and she started screaming her head off like an insane person. I was beyond angry and seriously thought it was going to get physical. Tanya looked as if she was going to throw a punch at any moment. Instinctively, I backed away from Tanya as quickly as I could, got in my car and drove off. I could not believe her fucking nerve. I was seconds away from assaulting this woman or probably defending myself from her assault and let's face it, she would win, she is a former marine after all.

All the way home I was super pissed off at this horrible person and shaking, literally shaking with rage. I was dwelling on what had transpired and going over it in my mind, getting more and more worked up thinking of what I might have said and considering the idea that I should have just told her I was going to meet her there and then blown it off. Let her still be waiting in the rain for her $12.50. I can't stop thinking about how super pissed off I am and then, suddenly, I'm reminded of Joy.

Still wet as I pull into my parking garage, I laugh, take a deep breath and let it all go.

Lily

# Pet Psycho

Professional pet sitters have responsibilities that need to be incorporated seamlessly into their clients' lives. Their work and diligence go unnoticed, unless there is an issue. In that sense, pet sitters are a bit like car mechanics; you don't really think about needing one until you do and then a good one can either make your life that much better or wreck it all together.

Over my many years as a professional pet sitter I have taken care of thousands of pets and slept over in countless client homes. While I'd like to brag that all my experiences have been seamless, that would be a lie. I've had dogs escape while under my supervision, (thank goodness I found her), been bitten a few times, got locked out (of a client's home) and locked in (which is actually more terrifying). I've been videotaped without permission (pretty sure), have had clients yell at me, bamboozle me and even insult me. I even had a client dump her dog on me (I found him a good home).

I've tried to be diplomatic with clients whose treatment of their pets was bordering on abuse and I've called the authorities when I believed the pets were being abused. Through all these experiences I have tried my best to remain professional, do what is best for the pet, safeguard my reputation and follow the golden rule of doing unto others as I would want done to me. Countless times I have given a client a raving review of their pet after I boarded them, not having the heart to tell them their furry friend crapped in my living room or their little sweetheart tried to bite my son. I've remained patient as clients have ruined my dinner plans by running late to retrieve their pets and went along when clients wanted to drop off at 5a.m. because they don't want to pay for the previous nights cost of boarding. I've spent countless nights kept awake by barking, crying and whimpering. I've had clients make unrealistic demands and then refuse to pay for *any* service when their unrealistic request cannot be performed (I can't train your dog in one day.) I had a particular client, a man, insist he wanted to hide in the closet while I was staying at his home to see if his dog could really smell that he was there.

I agreed to a test run of this (I 'm a people pleaser). Turns out, just as I suspected, the dog knew he was there right away. Imagine! While my instincts told me not to go for this, my sense of good client relations, made me give it a try.

Maintaining good client relationships along with providing excellent pet care will yield any pet sitter plenty of work. Pet sitting can be an evergreen profession, allowing the pet sitter to have repeat business throughout her career as long as she so chooses. Unfortunately, it's not always up to us, the pet sitter, which jobs we get and which ones we don't get.

I had a client who habitually rescued and rehabilitated the least adoptable dogs. The dogs had been rescued from extreme situations of abuse and in some cases sadistic animal cruelty and even torture.

I admired my client, Crystal, for her charity and her willingness to adopt these unadoptable dogs, thought to be ruined. She was a wealthy, single woman who spared no expense when it came to her house, her wardrobe or her dog. Crystal was constantly looking to connect more with her dogs and gain insights into their experiences so she could better understand them and any issues they might be having. In addition to hiring the best dog trainers, Crystal also sought assistance from a Hollywood pet psychic.

Crystal and I had a tepid relationship, at best. She was guarded around people and seemed to only open up to her dogs and her closest friends. I was neither. I had house sat for her on a few occasions, but had never gotten any feedback from her whether she was happy with my service or not. I assumed she was happy or why would she continue to call upon me? The dog certainly seemed to like me and I thought the dog was just fine, showing no signs of aggression, which can be an issue with dogs from these backgrounds.

The dog's name was Jasmine; she was a rescued pit bull that had been used as a bait dog. She seemed to have come out of it okay, now living literally in the lap of luxury. This dog was better off than me; she had flown first class all around the world, along side Crystal, on more than one occasion. I was looking forward to an extended stay at Crystal's house while she traveled to Europe. Crystal had a mansion in a historical part of Los Angeles called Hancock Park, the neighborhood was full of history from the bygone era of old Hollywood glamour and I was looking forward to moving in if only for a short time. Crystal called me about a month before she was to leave on her trip so we could, "talk about things." I was practically packing my bags.

We sat there, the four of us. The pet psychic, Jasmine, my client and me. I wasn't anticipating that the pet psychic would be there, Crystal hadn't mentioned it, but I embraced it anyway. I was open to the experience and even interested in what she had to say.

I had had my own interesting experience with a pet psychic and my dog, Dexter. This particular pet psychic had come to my home and "read" Dexter. She told me pretty much everything I already knew from the rescue and went on to tell me that Dexter *really* loves me. "Of course he loves me," I said, "I saved his life."

"No, no, he *really* loves you, in a romantic way." I looked over at Dexter, who was sitting on the couch across from me, just staring at me. Suddenly it occurred to me that he stares at me a lot.

"Dexter says if he was a human he would marry you and take you away from all this."

"He wants you to know that his love for you is deep."

I considered what the pet psychic said about Dexter loving me and after that I stopped letting him see me naked. Dexter would always sit outside the bathroom door when I was showering or even lay up against the bathtub if I was having a bath. He always seemed to be right there if any undressing was going on. I started to think maybe Dexter is a pervert and since there was no way to tell for sure, I'd better just start playing it safe. Besides, if he really loves me like that, there's no point in torturing him.

This pet psychic communicating with Jasmine is completely different, an entirely different vibe. If she tells Crystal that Jasmine loves her in a romantic way I will be shocked.

Jasmine was sneaking dirty looks in my direction…were those dirty looks or just my imagination?

"Hmm," the psychic was saying and nodding her head, "hmmm, really," and more head nodding. I looked at Jasmine, we made eye contact and then she looked away.

Initially, I believed that the psychic was actually getting communications from Jasmine. The psychic was able to collaborate what the rescue agency had told Crystal, that Jasmine had previously been treated horribly and that she had given birth to puppies, which had died. Jasmine communicated her sad story to the psychic and I admit, it was awful. She had been forced to fight her friends and was beaten and tortured. I was feeling really awful for her. Poor thing.

Jasmine went on communicating about herself and her life nonstop to the psychic. Clearly, she had a lot to say and the psychic was relaying all this information to us. All feelings of doubt in the psychic's abilities faded away as the psychic relayed hours of information, most of which we already knew.

Jasmine was sprawled out on an overstuffed couch, which looked out at the fountains in the garden. I sat across from her on a round ottoman, my back to the pool. The psychic sat comfortably in a swivel chair while Crystal was curled up on the couch with Jasmine. We were surrounded by baskets of dog toys, which went untouched as we clung to the psychic's words.

Crystal was torn between leaving Jasmine at home with me or taking her with her. She really couldn't decide, she had been struggling with the decision and had approached the pet psychic for spiritual guidance.

I liked Jasmine well enough. She was aloof, for a dog, and set in her own ways. She was very much like Crystal, independent and snooty.

I didn't know the psychic's back story, who she was, where she came from or what her credentials were. But, Crystal had asked me to join in and I thought it would be a great experience.

The psychic asked Jasmine how it made her feel when Crystal traveled and left me to take care of her. Jasmine turned her head away from me. The psychic would speak to us and then mentally "speak" to Jasmine.

I tried to think of what, if anything, Jasmine could say to incriminate me. Okay, maybe I didn't walk her as much as she would have liked, maybe I wasn't heating her gourmet dog food to the exact right temperature, maybe I didn't always let her watch her television shows. I wasn't perfect. But, I thought, I was the perfect pet sitter. Jasmine wanted for nothing while I watched her, perhaps I had given her too many treats and smothered her with too much attention and affection, I was doing my best.

The psychic looked at me and nodded in my direction. I was ready for her to heap on the praise. "Jasmine is not comfortable with you here." The psychic spoke these words and at first, I thought she was directing them at Crystal. It took me a moment to realize that Jasmine was not comfortable with *me*.

"What?" I said. "Me, why, what did I do?"

More nodding on the psychic's part.

"Jasmine says that you stole her boyfriend...in the last lifetime."

They all looked at me.

"I see," I said, taking it in slowly. I didn't know how to respond but felt certain of my innocence. I started to get a sinking feeling in my stomach. I longed to redirect the conversation to more current affairs but sensed that train had already left the station.

Digging my butt further into the ottoman, which was now starting to hurt my back, I gave the statement from the psychic some thought. Her words swirled in the living room air as Crystal looked at me intensely, her head tilted. Clearly, I had to volley back the bomb the psychic had just dropped in my lap.

"According to *my* psychic, I was a lesbian in that lifetime, it really couldn't have been me."

I had to fight the crazy with crazy. I was proud of myself for coming up with something so outlandish so quickly. For a second, I believed it myself.

The psychic was nodding more. Jasmine hopped off the couch and left the living room. We could hear her lapping up water in the kitchen.

I wasn't sure how much of this shit Crystal was going to buy. But I didn't want to lose my opportunity to stay in Crystal's home for a few months while she was gone.

"Is there anything Jasmine can add about this *current* lifetime, something that speaks to my abilities as a pet care provider or house sitter? Maybe Jasmine would like to comment on the quality of the time I spend with her?" Or those smelly farts I don't call her out on.

The psychic spoke directly to Crystal, completely ignoring me. I could see where this was going. My psychic abilities are giving me a message that the psychic is also a pet and house sitter. I knew it!

The psychic had Crystal in the palm of her hand. She could make up anything and I could do nothing about it.

Stole her boyfriend in another lifetime? Who could believe such horseshit?

Crystal and the Psycho were looking at me. My goose was cooked.

Crystal got up first. I could tell she was going to escort me out, no need to tell me she was going in another direction. We got to the front door and stopped.

"You know what, Crystal?" Our eye contact was uncomfortable.

I didn't know what I was going to say, but I knew I had to make it good. I thought to tell her I wasn't psychic but that I was intuitive and my intuition told me the psychic was full of crap.

Instead, I went out the door and stood on the top step, unmoving, as I waited for some last words to come to me. I stepped down one step, turned and looked back at Crystal.

"Don't believe everything you hear."

Not my best, but it was succinct.

Back in my car, I looked up at the house. Jasmine was in the bay window, settled on her padded perch, where she sat in judgment of the world as it went by.

I looked up at her, knowing it was the last time we'd see each other.

As I drove away, she grinned at me.

# Celebrity Treatment

Most pet sitters offer overnight stays in their client's home. This is perfect for the client that wants to travel but would like their pets to remain at home. I think this is the best scenario for most pets. Not all, but most. The pets can stay at home where they feel the most comfortable and the clients can travel knowing someone is staying at their house, taking care of things, caring for their pets and keeping an eye on their property.

Other people prefer boarding their pets. I also offer boarding in my home for dogs that are already clients or come by at least once and pass the "test." The "test" is not biting my face off, and of course, they have to get along with Dexter. Dexter is my dog and he has his own problems. Dexter is a rescue dog that was abused. Due to his past history he has developed fear aggression. Fear aggression is when the dog acts aggressively out of fear. We can be sitting at the kitchen table having a perfectly nice chat and all of sudden; Dexter will try and bite you as you stand up. I usually keep Dexter away from people but he can interact with other dogs. Some dogs don't like interaction with other dogs but love interacting with people. Dexter likes the dogs, but tries to bite the people. He is a real pain in the ass sometimes but I love him very much and would never re-home him or give him up. I just have to keep a really good eye on him so he doesn't bite anyone-again!

The majority of my over night visits with pets are typically with established clients. Some of these houses I've stayed at longer than I've lived at some of my own addresses.

When I first started Your Dog's Best Friend in the early 2000's I was single, had no dog, no young kid and was frankly excited about staying in other people's homes. Hollywood Hills, Malibu, Hidden Hills, yes, I stayed in all sorts of homes. Celebrities too! I used to love to practice award acceptance speeches with real Oscars, Emmys and Grammys. I would use the pools, sleep in amazing beds, and be tasked with driving luxury cars like Maserati's so they wouldn't go into disrepair while the clients were away and it was all very exciting and fun. Sure, it was fun. Occasionally. More than that though, it was and is a huge responsibility. Rich and famous people have more things and all those things need taking care of and looking after. It takes the fun out of lying by the pool when the housekeeper and nanny are lurking about.

During the spring of 2004 an assistant to a celebrity called and asked me if I was available for overnights. Normally she did the overnights but this time she would be traveling with her employer and they needed someone trustworthy who they could use again and again. People always say this. "We're going to need you all the time." What they really mean is, *we're only going to use you this one time, but we want you to think we'll be calling you again, so you'll do an amazing job...this one time.*

I went to meet with the client and her assistant at her gorgeous home in Beverly Hills. She had a pool and a tennis court. And a delightful Lhasa Apso named Gizmo. The dog was darling! Really cute and adorable and smelled like lavender. Surely, the dog came with a high price tag from a breeder but I didn't care. It was obvious the celebrity was in love with her dog, and the dog was her most prized possession. I bonded with the celebrity immediately over the fact that her dog is the *cutest dog ever*! The assistant is wordless during all of this. The celebrity is French kissing the dog. She is making baby noises and making out with the dog, they're so in love. The assistant stands by and watches all this but says nothing. I can sense some tensions between her and the celebrity.

Finally, the celebrity tells the assistant, "Hire her and take care of it." Gizmo jumps all over me and smothers me with kisses. I can tell the dog knows I'm a dog person because she is super excited that I'm there. The celebrity leaves the room and carries Gizmo out with her.

The assistant turned to me and said, "No people over!"

"Absolutely," I said back immediately. I act equally aghast by this suggestion.

And, "No smoking in the house." I nod my agreement.

The assistant seems thrilled to be giving out orders instead of taking them and gives me a complicated schedule for Gizmo. Gizmo needs her food at exactly this time and temperature. Gizmo eats twenty pieces of kibble at each meal with three measured tablespoons of shredded fresh roasted chicken. No skin. I am to go to the market and buy the freshest rotisserie chicken I can find. Only named-brand biscuits as treats. (As if Gizmo would know.) Teeth brushed every night. Hair brushed every night. I'm used to all this. There is nothing new, here's the special dog toothbrush with the liver toothpaste to brush her teeth. Here's the Tiffany dog brush, etc.

The assistant is going on and on about Gizmo's needs. I've been here approaching two hours for no pay and I need to wrap it up. I'm tired, hungry, thirsty, and I want to go home. I've been dog walking since six a.m. this morning; it's now almost six-thirty at night and I got here at four. The sweat on my shirt has dried and I begin to fantasize about showering. "So," the assistant says, "you see, because it's human hair, it has to be brushed out completely everyday." Wait! I missed something. "What's human hair?" I say, snapping to attention? "Gizmo's," she says, completely normally. "Gizmo has human hair?"

"Yes, she's hypoallergenic and doesn't shed because she has human hair."

"Gizmo has human hair?" I keep saying it so it might dawn on her how ridiculous this statement actually is. "Is there a problem?" she asks me.

She's sitting here telling me the dog has human hair and then asks me if there is a problem. The argumentative side of me, which is a big side, really wants to be right and prove to this imbecile that the dog cannot have human hair.

It is impossible for a dog to have human hair. In fact some dogs have hair like humans, they don't have fur, they have hair instead of fur but to be sure, it is not human hair.

"Is it a wig?" "Is it a wig made with human hair?" I have to know what the hell is going on with the dog with the human hair. "So, did the dog have human hair from birth?" I ask, "Because the dog has been bred with a…human?" The assistant is irritated with me. I suspect that she herself had been told that the dog has human hair and she accepted that as a fact and then turned around and repeated it to me, and I was like WHAT? I wrap it up by telling her it's interesting, really interesting and I can't wait to brush Gizmo, with the human hair.

She writes me a check for ten days. We work out the details, when to arrive, when to leave and of course Gizmo's schedule. Gizmo has a very detailed schedule. What Gizmo will be happy to learn is that she will be sleeping most of the time I am staying there because I have real dogs to walk with real dog fur and real dog poops.

Finally, I can leave. It's a quarter to seven. My college admission interview took less time.

The assistant gives me the remote control for the garage. No house key, just the clicker and the alarm code. I'm happy to leave. I've got to get home, shower and eat and run up to Malibu to spend the night with Max, the retired show dog. Thankfully Max has a dog door so he's not waiting for me to let him out. He'll just want dinner and company, when you think about it, dogs aren't so different from us, are they?

The following Sunday I drove over to Gizmo's house in Beverly Hills. I'm happy to be staying there; I'll be a little closer to my clientele. I pull into the garage. There is a BMW convertible and a Range Rover. I swear every house in Beverly Hills must come with a Range Rover. I wonder if the convertible is the assistant's? No, they probably took her car to the airport. I decide I don't care and I don't. The celebrity can have two cars. Fine. I Just want to go inside and see Gizmo.

I go through the door to the inside. I am staying in the room off the garage, right next to the kitchen. The ironing board is set up. There is a twin bed. I look around the house. Where is Gizmo? I had assumed Gizmo would be jumping up and down, excited to have company. She was a very friendly and excitable dog. I had only met her once but knew enough to know she should be right there at the door. I mean that's dog 101. Greet person at door.

I don't see or hear Gizmo anywhere. I'm calling out Gizmo's name and can hear her whimpering but can't see her. I open the door to the celebrity bedroom and my jaw hits the floor. It is the most gorgeous room I've ever seen in my life. All white. Everything is white. Round bed, glass furniture, white framed art, all overlooking her eternity pool. I instantly want to stay in there but know better.

More whimpering…I follow the sound into the walk-in closet. The closet is bigger than any closet I've seen. Don't think about that I tell myself. You are providing a valuable service and giving this woman peace of mind by taking care of her beloved…dog! And there, in the back of the closet, like last years Gucci, is Gizmo.

Oh my god! I cannot believe that she would leave Gizmo here at the back of her closet like this! I open the crate and of course Gizmo comes flying out. I pick her up and carry her out of the closet and out of the bedroom. I don't give any of the gorgeous clothes a second look. I'm thinking what a phony the celebrity is. Why didn't she leave the dog in the kitchen or really would it have killed her to leave the dog in my room? I'm thinking this was a bitchy move on the part of the assistant but maybe she just keeps her dog in there?

Who knows?

While they were gone, the house was under construction. No one told me this was going to happen, so I woke up on Monday morning to the sound of jackhammers breaking up the old patio in the yard. The house painters showed up, too. Apparently, the assistant was supposed to coordinate some specifics on choosing exterior paint colors.

In no time, I had picked out the colors for the exterior of the house and coordinating trim. For their part, the painters never knew I wasn't the assistant. I suppose, to them, if you've seen one blonde, you've seen them all.

Throughout my entire stay at the celebrity's house, it was a beehive of activity. The mobile groomer came without warning; the assistant never said she was scheduled. Fresh flower arrangements were delivered twice in the same week. Someone came to tune the piano, mobile car washers showed up and cleaned the already spotless cars and meal delivery service coolers stacked up by the front door. The assistant had been so busy going on about the dog and her human hair; she forgot to mention all the other things I would be left in charge of.

All week long, there was one surprise after another. Of course, I could never get a hold of the assistant to ask questions, I tried to make the best decisions I could. Had I known I was going to be responsible for so much more than Gizmo and the house, I would have charged more.

When the actress and her assistant finally returned, the house had been completely repainted with the colors I had chosen. The flowerbeds now held the flowers I liked and the meal delivery service was vegan. Gizmo and I had a grand time making these decisions together.

Every night I brushed Gizmo's hair and told her what a good dog she was before we would snuggle into bed together.

If they had been unhappy with my services, I'm sure I would have heard something.

But I never heard from them again.

# That's A Wrap

In spring 2004, I decided to get serious about marketing and advertising for Your Dog's Best Friend. The company had been growing organically through word of mouth and client referrals but I craved faster growth.

Pay per click advertising and Search Engine Optimization (SEO) weren't what they are today so there was little I could do on the internet except for having a website and using some broad search words and terms. I noticed a technique called "wrapping" was becoming a popular new trend in Hollywood, especially on cars. Wrapping is advertising on a piece of vinyl that is "wrapped" around your car, building or bus.

Once you've seen it, you notice it everywhere and can't stop seeing it.

The first car I saw wrapped was advertising "Red Bull" energy drink. They were using Volkswagen Beetles exclusively at the time to advertise and had even gone one-step further and added "wings" to some cars.

As I drove a Volkswagen myself, I investigated becoming a Red Bull advertiser. I spoke with the person at Red Bull in charge of hiring "affiliates" and picked his brain about how the program was working for Red Bull. He told me it had been an incredible campaign for them and had brought branding to the next level.

All I needed was a Beetle, and to commit a certain amount of time to going to sporting events and handing out Red Bull. I can't remember how much it paid but it was a few hundred extra dollars a month.

I thought about taking on the Red Bull commitment to earn extra money but then thought to myself, *Hey, why advertise for them when I can be advertising for Your Dog's Best Friend (YDBF)?* It didn't make sense to want to brand YDBF and gain more business but then drive a "Red Bull" vehicle. Immediately, I traded my Beetle for a Toyota Highlander. I didn't want to confuse any potential clients by having the same style of car as another Beetle advertiser. Plus, I realized it wasn't practical to transport dogs in the Beetle anymore; it was time to get serious about the dog business.

The logo for YDBF is a cartoon girl walking a bunch of dogs with a big grin on her face. I call her Ellen after Ellen DeGeneres because I think she looks super friendly and approachable even though she is only a cartoon. I had the computer files created to wrap my vehicle and went in search of a company that could get the job done but not charge me too much. I eventually decided on a place in Burbank that operated not far from where I used to live when I first moved to LA.

I met with the owner several times and decided on a yellow wrap background with my orange multi-color logo overlaid. I had so many colors on the logo that they had to charge me extra. The owner used computer software to show me exactly how my car would look like once it was done. If "Red Bull" gives you wings, Your Dog's Best Friend was going to give you woofs! It looked amazing!

Figuring I was going to get lots of business from the wrap, I purchased an 800 number that would be easy to catch if you happened to be driving by. Because the URL for my website is long, I wanted people to instantly grab the name of my business so potential clients could easily contact me.

This was definitely one of the best business decisions I had ever made and I couldn't wait to begin getting more clients. Sitting in my car that night I was overwhelmed with potential and excitement. I knew the wrap was going to perform exactly how I hoped.

In anticipation of all the incoming calls, I hired a separate phone operator to answer over flow calls. I set her up at my house in my home office at my computer. The 800 number would bounce to my cell phone and then if my line was busy, she would have the calls routed to her. I was so excited! Despite the fact I hadn't gotten much sleep the night before, I couldn't wait to get in my vehicle the next morning and drive. I had gone to the office supply store and hooked up the passenger seat in my car with notebooks and folders and office supplies to take notes. I also had Bluetooth installed so I could safely talk and drive at the same time. Pulling out of my driveway that morning I felt like a contestant on "Dancing With the Stars", who had consumed too much caffeine.

Normally I'm on autopilot in my car but that morning was different. I made eye contact with the other drivers to see if anyone noticed. I paid attention to see if any of my neighbors might be leaving for work at the same time so they could check me out, but none of them did. When I got on the 101 Freeway to head to Santa Monica to pick up my first clients I felt giddy. I literally could not wait for the phone to start ringing.

A busload of school kids rode next to me and waved. I noticed that because Ellen was so friendly looking, a lot of kids waved at me. Excitedly, I waved back to them. I felt like a celebrity. It was getting noticed but no one was calling. This was more than a little frustrating. The wrap had cost me a couple thousand dollars and I wanted to see some return on my investment sooner rather than later.

I pulled into the homeowner's gate where I picked up Norman and Millie, Labrador retrievers I walked every day. The guard noticed but didn't say anything. Typical, I thought, *maybe these Hollywood types are trained not to remark on the obvious*. You know, like facelifts. I got out of my car beaming with pride and went into the house to collect the dogs. If they had noticed they certainly didn't show it.

I let Norman and Millie hang their heads out of the car window taking extra pride in noticing that their presence added to the authenticity of the advertising. Norman, a gorgeous black lab, my favorite dog ever, looked almost identical to one of the cartoon dogs. And Millie, a white lab, who always looked like she was smiling. It was perfect.

I drove Norman and Millie to the neighborhoods of Santa Monica where I usually walked them not too far from the ocean. They hung out of the car with big grins on their faces, I kept looking at my phone but the only person who called was my sister from New York to see how it was going. I told her I couldn't talk and hung up. I was surprised no one had called, but what could I do? After about an hour of walking Norman and Millie we returned to my car and I gave them some water from out of the portable water bowls I kept in the back. They drank and laid down to rest in the back seat. I turned the car on and started driving up and down the residential streets of Santa Monica. The car was basically a rolling advertisement so I drove slowly and aimlessly. The song, "No Particular Place to Go" by Chuck Berry played in my head and I hummed a few bars.

I didn't have to return Norman and Millie for a while so I took in the sights of Santa Monica: the manicured lawns, the beautiful houses, the greenery and scenery. I was anxious that no one had called or noticed the wrap but I took deep breaths and repeated "patience" to myself over and over. It was my mantra and generally I felt happy. I loved Norman and Millie so much. They were the most wonderful labs. I am one of those people who think of dogs as humans on the inside and relate to them like I would humans, even having conversations with them and giving them their own voices so they can respond.

I did a few loops up and down Montana Avenue, as that's the main shopping area. Santa Monica is a tony beach town located on the west side of Los Angeles; it's full of wealthy, beautiful, and entitled people. I reached one particular street, Carlyle, and pulled my car into a shaded spot, I intentionally parked in this spot because it was shady and a nice street to pull over in and make some calls. Parts of the street were sunny but I positioned my car between patches of sun so I could roll down the windows and chill for a few minutes before taking the dogs home. Once we were parked and settled I called my house on the landline and let the operator go. She seemed disappointed after only working a few hours but I explained that while I was disappointed, too, there seemed no need for her to sit there.

*It's just a matter of time*, I thought to myself, while staring at my phone, willing it to ring. I looked over my shoulder at Norman who was sprawled on the back seat. He gave me a big smile and thumped his tail. Millie was sitting up next to him, smiling and panting. They both looked so happy. We had walks and water and soon they'd be back at their loving home in one of the swankiest canyons off Sunset Boulevard. Lucky dogs!

I find that most people have the same breed of dogs as they had in their childhood. I had two black labs growing up; Ginger first, and King much later, after Ginger had been gone for a while. It took my parents years to recover from losing her to old age and they even said they would never get another dog but then one day my mother went to Chicago's Anti-Cruelty Society and surprised us by bringing home a puppy.

In January 1986, I stayed home from high school with a terrible cold. That was the day the Space Shuttle exploded on live TV, so I'll probably never forget it. My parents rarely allowed us to watch television, especially daytime TV. They said TV was for losers and a big waste of time. This morning, my mother told me she was going out but didn't say where. Rarely did my parents leave us alone in the house as they worried that "something" might happen. My mother instructed me to watch an educational show so I lay on the couch and watched the long and boring introduction into what would become the Space Shuttle launch.

My family had one very large tube television as this was before the days of flat screens, widescreens or high definition. The television was more than a television; it was a huge piece of furniture and its surface had a large space, which we used as a catchall of sorts. We had crap piled on top of it, but the TV guide was always right on top. There was no remote. You had to get up and change the channel manually or sit on the carpet in front of the television and turn the dials around.

I was waiting for the countdown and finally it began; 10, 9, 8, 7, 6, 5, 4, 3, 2, 1 Blastoff! The shuttle accelerated a short distance off the ground and then it exploded. Just like that. I blinked at the screen trying to make sense of it. How could that have happened? My mother was on the screen now, her dark shadow taking over the space on the tube, coming in out of the brutal Chicago cold. She walked over to me with a grin and placed a warm bundle wrapped in a blue baby blanket on my lap.

For an instant I think it might be a baby. Suddenly, I realized it was a puppy, which by now had worked his way out of the blanket and began licking and chewing on me. He has that delicious freshly hatched puppy smell. I started kissing him, quickly forgetting that the shuttle had just crashed. My mother went to hang her coat in the front closet turning the TV off on her way. I watched the long horizontal death of the television tube, as the screen line turned to a dot and disappeared and the screen went blank. My mom bringing King home that day was as unexpected as the Space Shuttle exploding.

Ginger, our first black Lab whom my father had brought home had been my childhood best friend but King, was my mother's dog. She brought him home on that fateful day and she was his mommy from then on. In 1990, my mother passed away from colon cancer at the age 50. King outlived her by many years and when he eventually died it felt like my mother had died all over again. Perhaps I am in the dog business as a way of reconnecting to that unconditional love I felt from my dogs in my childhood? When it didn't matter that a great tragedy had just unfolded, as long as there was a warm fur ball in my lap.

Fast-forward eighteen years, as I sat in my parked car on a beautiful day in sunny Santa Monica. I was still getting used to being in the car with the wrap. The tiny pinholes that made up the wrap, which covered the windows, were easier to see out of than I thought they would be.

I was shuffling my business cards around and re-arranging my notebooks while drinking some water in the air-conditioned car when I noticed a woman coming out of her house striding purposefully towards me. This was it! The first person to inquire about my services because of the wrap! I was so thrilled; my heart was beating in anticipation. I hoped she wanted dog walking or maybe even house sitting. I took a deep breath, ready to make my pitch as professional and graceful as possible. I rolled down my window and gave her my biggest smile as I excitedly said "Hi!"

As I was about to hand her my business card she said to me in a very nasty voice: "Can you move your van?" She pretty much demanded it. No hello or niceties, she just marched out of her house and asked me to move my car. I was more than a bit startled and I remember looking at her with an 'I don't compute' look on my face. "Look" she went on, "I don't want people to think there's no one home at my place and rob me because you're parked out here with a van that says 'housesitting' on it."

Which really didn't make any sense, just because my car says 'housesitting' on it does not necessarily mean I am housesitting your home. Just because the plumber is parked outside my house doesn't mean my toilet is backed up. I was trying to recover from the surprise but could see she was really fuming.

I didn't want to argue with her but I also didn't understand what her problem was. "Besides," she said, "you've got the whole street to park on, so why you have to park in front of my house with your tacky pet van is beyond me!" Then she spun around in her blue Juicy velour tracksuit and marched back into her house slamming the door behind her. I had not said anything but "hi!" throughout the entire conversation.

I was mortified. I could not believe that this woman had nothing better to do than to come out of her house and bust my balls for parking in front of her house and she called my car a van which it was not a van it was an SUV and she called it tacky and she was wearing a blue Juicy velour track suit. The matching pants and jacket. What a bitch!

As soon as she was back in her house Norman let out a loud bark. "Yeah Norman," I said to him, "why didn't you bite her?"

I questioned the entire Universe at that moment, which was disconcerting. I'm a big believer in angels and manifesting, so why, if I had the entire block to park had I chosen this woman's house? What was the lesson? I sat there for a few more seconds and thought that I had better get moving because she was probably in her house looking out of her spy window, waiting for me to leave.

I reflected on the experience while driving Millie and Norman home. I tried to let it go. But like the Space Shuttle exploding and King coming home the wrap would forever be associated with the memory of this unpleasant woman.

This occurrence reminded me of another time in this exact same neighborhood when a similar situation happened. I had been walking Norman and Millie and suddenly felt like there was another person on the walk with us. I turned and looked and sure enough another dog was marching along with us on the walk like, "hey don't mind me, I'm just here for the scenery." He seemed happy to be in our pack. Even Norman and Millie didn't seem to mind. I immediately panicked when I saw him. He was a beautiful dog, obviously someone's baby who was probably worried sick about him. I stopped walking and figured out a way to double leash Norman and Millie and use a leash on him. It was no small feat, putting two leashes on three dogs but I did it. I am nothing if not resourceful. I looked at the tags on the dogs collar, and called the number but it went to voice mail. I knew I had to get him home to save his owners from panicking.

I put Norman and Millie back in my car. The dog's tag said "Roscoe." Thank goodness he was wearing a collar. Nothing's worse than finding a stray without a collar. "Okay Roscoe, show me where you live, it has to be on this block, right?" I started knocking on doors and talking to people. I went up and down the entire street thinking surely the owner would appear at any minute looking for him. This was a beautiful yellow Lab, definitely from a breeder; he was well groomed and well mannered. Finally I rang the doorbell of a house Roscoe kept eyeballing, and a young woman answered. She was on her cell phone saying, "Uh huh, ok, ok", so she obviously was not having a conversation about her missing dog. She swung the door wide open when she saw me standing there, nodded her head at Roscoe, and indicated at him to get inside, completely ignoring me. Roscoe shot me a parting look that read, "Thanks! It's been a slice," and he went inside with his tail held high. And then she shut the door in my face.

"You're welcome!" I screamed as loudly as I could. Not that I was expecting a reward or anything but a little appreciation would have been nice. I ran back to my car where Norman and Millie were standing on the seats wagging their tails.

"Can you believe that shit?" I said while getting back into my seat. But, of course, they didn't answer.

So here I was on another Santa Monica street feeling down. I started up my car and began driving back to Norman and Millie's to drop them off and then head to Bel Air to pick up more dogs. While I was driving along, finally the 800 number rang!

"Hello! Your Dog's Best Friend!" I answered enthusiastically.

"What do you charge for grooming?"

"Oh, we're not groomers. We're dog walkers and pet sitters."

Click. *Gosh, what is wrong with people?* I was getting bummed.

"All right, take it easy," I told myself. "This is the first day. It's unrealistic to think this is going to pay for itself on the first day. Lower your expectations." Seems like lowering my expectations was status quo since moving to Los Angeles.

On the way to Bel Air I stopped for an ice coffee in Brentwood and as I was walking back up to my vehicle I smiled! I had made an investment in advertising and marketing and it was going to pay off. Despite the first day not meeting my expectations, I still felt confident I would get some business from the wrap.

Next I had to go and walk two Miniature Schnauzers for a retired

Law University professor who lived near UCLA. He waited for me to drive up so he could let me in. He noticed the wrap immediately. "What are the legal ramifications of something like this?" he asked me.

I glared at him, confused. "You know," he said, "what's it going to do to your insurance rates? It's a commercial vehicle now; surely you informed your insurance company." In fact I had not informed my insurance company. In fact, last I spoke to them I told them I drove my car only for work and school but they didn't ask me if it was wrapped, and at the time it hadn't been. "You have to tell them," he said. "If you have an accident in this now, it's a big liability. Someone could sue you and come after your whole company. This is a pretty litigious society we live in. You don't want to get sued." He lectured me while walking around my entire vehicle pointing out air bubbles in the wrap.

"Okay, thanks," I told him, "really appreciate the free legal advice." He finally left after what seemed like an eternity and I went in to leash up Bark-y and Bite-y his yappy little dogs. While I was harnessing Bark-y, Bite-y bit me on the ass. *Goddamn it,* I thought as I rubbed my butt trying to see if he had made a hole in my yoga tights.

*Lawsuit,* I thought to myself, *there's your liability right there.*

I walked the dogs in the neighborhood and saw an elderly lady walking a small dog. She must have been one of the neighbors because I saw her all the time. Her dog was also a senior, waddling besides the elderly woman. They looked like a sweet pair, the woman in her housedress and slippers, and the fat grey Chihuahua panting besides her.

I decided to leave my comfort zone and offer her my services as a professional dog walker. I had the feeling that I needed to get out there and push the business.

I walked closer to her as her dog was sniffing around in the grass and Bark-y and Bite-y were doing the same. I tell her that her dog is adorable. I love fat, old dogs. Only I don't say it like that to her.

Finally, I casually mentioned that I was a professional dog walker. She seemed intrigued.

"How much is it to walk my dog?" she asked.

"Well, it's $25."

"A month?" she practically squealed in shock.

"Uhm, no, it's $25 per walk."

"My lord!" she gasped. "Does anyone pay that?"

"Yes!" "It's a valuable service." I told her I could be flexible for people on a fixed income.

And that was that.

After Bark-y and Bite-y were put safely in their crates I picked up the dogs at my next clients in Bel Air and drove to Comstock Park to walk them. As I was parking, a woman in a Lexus pulled in behind me and came running over to my driver's side window.

"Hi," I said just as enthusiastically as I could muster.

"Hi," she said back, "I'm a dog walker too and just wonder what you're charging for dog walks." We chatted for a while and I gave her a breakdown of my rates. We exchanged cards and then she drove away. I walked the two dogs through the park past the lawn bowlers and golfers, over by the playground and around again. My phone wasn't ringing but the sun was shining and I was doing what I loved, spending time with dogs, and being out-doors. I finished the walk and started walking back to my car to see a woman in a Mercedes was taking down my information.

"Hi," she said to me as I was putting the girls back in the car.

"Hey." I said. I tried to remain cool.

"Are you the owner of this company?"

While her question seemed possibly confrontational, I figured that if she had a complaint I might as well face it head on.

I put out my hand to shake hers and said, "Yes, I'm Laura, and this is my company, Your Dog's Best Friend. We do dog walking and pet sitting."

"Oh great," she said, "do you service the Bel Air area?" I told her we did! She asked me how much it would cost to walk her Malti-poo and I quoted her a rate; we talked for a while longer and I booked an appointment with her the next day. I drove away feeling ecstatic. The woman, Holly, turned out to be one of my best clients and meeting her meant the wrap ended up paying for itself, with her business alone.

I drove back to Bel Air on cloud nine. So now I could see and even accept that, some people would notice and some people wouldn't but it would definitely help my business.

I dropped the girls in Bel Air and headed up the canyon to Studio City and Sherman Oaks to walk some more dogs. On the way up the canyon the 800 number rang again, "Hello, Your Dog's Best Friend, this is Laura, how can I help you?"

"Laura sweetheart, can you drive your car faster? I'm behind you on the canyon and you're going too slow." Sure enough, I looked in my rear view mirror and there was this guy in a Porsche riding on my ass super fast. You know the type. He waved to me when I saw him. I pulled over so he could pass.

I walked a few more dogs in the valley and then I had to run some errands at the mall in Sherman Oaks. When I arrived there was no parking. I drove up and down the aisles looking for a spot when a woman in a station wagon driving the wrong way on the aisle yelled at me, "Get out of the way in your fucking doggie van!"

I smiled back at her, flashed the peace sign, and yelled back, "It's not a van, it's a SUV."

I had the wrap on my car with my phone number on it for more than five years and I fielded all sorts of calls. When you drive around with your phone number on your car you open yourself up to an unknown world where anything can happen.

Perverts called, people complained about my driving, and children always waived. Friends saw me but I didn't see them. I had no anonymity. I joked with people that I could no longer do any undercover work. Sometimes clients thought it wasn't such a good idea to have the wrap on the car and asked me to park up the street if I was staying at their house, and I always accommodated them.

I did get a lot of business from the wrap, so the return on the investment was good. To this day I believe having the wrap was one of the best decisions I ever made for YDBF and it gave me lots of memorable experiences.

# Your Dog Died

Dogs give us unconditional love. This kind of love, completely devoid of betrayal and judgment, rarely exists between humans. Dogs are our furry children; we baby them and we pamper them. We can't stand the thought of losing them, and we don't want them to die. As a professional pet sitter being paid to care for your dog, I *really* don't want your dog to die. That's like losing two clients at once. The loss is felt twice as hard.

For me, the dog is the customer, and the human just happens to write the checks. I get to know your dog in a special way. We create a bond. When the dog sees me, he knows we're going for a walk or to do something fun. I love all the dogs like they are my own. I've taken care of puppies, dogs with three legs and in wheel chairs, dogs that have been abused, dogs adopted from other countries, and dogs that survived on the streets. I once took care of a rescue dog, a beagle mix that some monster had wrapped barbed wire around his mouth to shut him up.

Most dogs are from breeders, shelters or rescues, and frankly I don't care where you get them as long as you take care of them. And that means to the end.

I've been there with my human clients while they've put their dogs to sleep. I cried with my very good client who let her springer spaniel out for one minute, while she collected a pizza at the door, and he got run over and killed by the neighbors speeding teenager. I've seen dogs age and get sick, and I've listened to their owners agonize over putting them to sleep. When is it too soon? Maybe we waited too long?

I have become accustomed to the scheduling of the final shot, the black mark on the calendar, the last trip to the vet, the human deciding when the end should be. I completely blanked on the fact that a dog can just die.

And this is exactly what happened. I never saw it coming.

Ralph was a 17-year-old golden retriever. He was the furry son to a couple with grown daughters. Both the husband and wife were successful corporate attorneys; they lived in one of the swankiest gated communities in Los Angeles. I had been their dog sitter for a few years and knew Ralph well. This was the first time I was staying at their house while they traveled and I was looking forward to it.

At my initial meet and greet with Shelley and Marty they asked me so many questions I had to double check that Ralph was a dog and not an actual human. They were that concerned. Shelley later told me that she hired me because I was the only pet-sitter she interviewed who got down and petted her dog. How could I not? I've never met a mean or aggressive golden retriever. They are generally the sweetest things and Ralph was no exception. He was a beautiful specimen; something even old age couldn't take away from him. Ralph had a gorgeous shiny coat and beautiful pearly whites, which Shelley made me promise to brush twice a day.

(I don't recommend you try tasting the liver-flavored toothpaste for dogs, in case you were curious.)

All the puppy nonsense, chewing things up and zooming around the house was long over. Now Ralph simply smiled a lot and followed Shelley from room to room looking up at her with the most beautiful liquid eyes framed by long, faded eyelashes.

Shelley was Ralph's Mommy. Not his Mom, his Mommy. Her daughters had grown up and moved away so Ralph was her only remaining child. You might even say Shelley was borderline obsessed with Ralph. Maybe because she feared the inevitable.

Shelley had prepared a very lawyerly binder full of Ralph's care instructions. Doctors and various specialists, acupuncturists and groomers, Ralph had it all and more. Frankly I was a little jealous of Ralph.

Shelley had meticulously accounted for every possible scenario that might occur while I was with Ralph. Well, almost.

Shelley spent hours showing me how everything in the house worked including demonstrating how to retrieve the mail (they had a locked box at the end of their driveway), and dimming the high-tech light switches. If anyone had witnessed this, they would have sworn Shelley was a manic realtor who was showing me the house. At any moment I expected her to tell me the square footage and asking price. It finally ended when Marty called out from his den, "She can figure out how to work the damn light switches."

We fake smiled at each other.

I figured Marty probably just wanted to eat dinner, which was being held up by this "tour." I did not interact much with Marty. It was obvious Shelley was in charge.

Shelley stopped the tour at the crappiest room in the house and told me I would be sleeping in there. It was the servant's quarters. All big houses have that one crappy room where the weird uncle sleeps when he visits. This was that room. Instead of a walk-in closet, this room had a washer and dryer.

Shelley told me I had to squeegee the shower door after every shower. Although I thought this was strange, I told her I would. Just when I thought that was the end of that, Shelley proceeded to climb into the shower stall and demonstrate the proper technique. She slightly bent her legs up and down as she demonstrated running the rubber blade over her glass shower doors. She seemed to enjoy doing it but it looked hard on her knees. I stood and watched Shelley's tan Gucci loafers in the shower.

*She must think I'm an idiot.*

When she was finished with the squeegee demonstration, Shelley climbed out of the shower stall and explained that Ralph would be most comfortable in there with me and that's why they put me in the crappy room off the garage. *Bullshit,* I thought, *Ralph sleeps in the master bedroom where you sleep, you're not fooling me. You just want to give me this shitty room because you don't want me to stay in any of the other seven bedrooms, and you see me like a servant, someone you begrudgingly pay for a service.* I understood that.

"Besides, Marty has to carry him upstairs lately and we don't want you to have to do that." For this I was grateful because the house was huge. The daughters' bedrooms upstairs were each the size of my apartment and they didn't even live there anymore. One of them was getting married that weekend.

Shelley yelled at Marty to bring Ralph's bed into the bedroom. "Getting it!" he yelled back.

Ralph stood in the middle of the room glancing around nervously. I went over to him and petted him. "You're such a sweetheart, Ralphie, you're going to be a good boy, right?" He was panting and looking anxious. I know that panting can be a sign of pain in dogs and I hoped he wasn't in any pain. "He knows we're going away," Shelley said. "He saw the suitcases." "I wish you could come with us, Ralph." Shelley seemed to be apologizing to the dog for leaving him behind. Ralph was taking it well, blinking at me and giving me a slow tail wag.

They were going to Hawaii, as their oldest daughter was getting married there. I wondered if they would let me move into her room. Not just while they were away on the trip but permanently. I imagined living with Shelley and Marty and Ralph.

I really wanted that room. The daughter had decorated it like a Manhattan style apartment with art-deco furniture and hot pink walls. She had a closet full of designer clothes, a sunken Jacuzzi tub and plush carpeting.

I pictured myself living there, doing everyone's laundry and squeegeeing all the showers everyday. I guess I would have other responsibilities there. I was mulling it over, this imaginary deal, the things I would and would not agree to do, when Marty finally appeared at the servant quarters with Ralph's bed.

It looked like it weighed 100 pounds from the way it was crushing Marty. Ralph wagged his tail when he saw it.

Marty dropped it next to my bed and immediately; Ralph walked over to it, got in and fell asleep. After sizing up both beds, I quickly realized that Ralph's was undoubtedly the more comfortable of the two. It was a luxury dog bed made with a memory-foam lining and feather-soft padding. Two or three children could easily fit into it. I'm sure it had cost a fortune and was designed by some world-renowned canine orthopedic specialist. My bed, on the other hand, looked lumpy, even with the expensive duvet thrown on top.

To say that Ralph was spoiled would be a huge understatement. That would be like saying J.K. Rowling has "kind of" made it as a writer or that Elton John has "kind of" made it as a singer.

Ralph had had not one but two open-heart surgeries performed by Los Angeles' best surgeons. Medicines and therapies were keeping him alive and he took no less than twelve drugs each day. Ralph was frail and shaky. Still, he managed to get up most of the time and follow Shelley from room to room. There was no reason for me to think Ralph wasn't going to make it through the weekend.

Shelley was a little dynamo herself and ran the household and Marty, like a miniature army. Shelley went to Ralph's side and hugged him. Ralph looked over at me. He had the sweetest looking face but he looked a little sad. It was easy to see how much Shelley and Marty loved him.

Marty pointed again to the bag of golf clubs waiting outside my room, next to the garage. "Remember to grab one of the clubs when you walk Ralph." Marty showed me one of the irons and told me it was probably the best to use. They all looked the same to me but I agreed to never walk Ralph without a golf club. They were going to be damned if they spent a fortune keeping Ralph alive and then have a coyote get him while he was out on his walk. And Ralph was never to go in the yard unattended. Not for a second.

"And only walk him in the cul-de-sac," Shelley repeated for the millionth time. "Yes. Got it." I told them. They had probably spent more money on Ralph in his lifetime than my parents had spent on me.

Shelley and Marty loved Ralph like the son they never had. They would spare no expense to be sure he was comfortable, well cared for and around forever. I can't say that I blamed them. They earned massive amounts of money, and if they wanted to spend it on their dog why shouldn't they?

Shelley walked me to the impressive double front doors, still giving me last minute instructions. As I walked down her path to the front gate she called after me. "Do you remember how to push the button to get out?" I shot her back my best withering look; I wanted to yell back at her that, "Yes! I remember how to push the button." Some of it was infuriatingly insulting.

The next morning I arrived at Ralph's house at 5 a.m. in order to see Shelley and Marty off to Hawaii and to make sure Ralph didn't spend a minute alone. Typically I never agree to this. I usually show up a few hours later when they are safely on the plane. There is no need for me to be there when my clients leave unless they are completely and hopelessly neurotic.

I only agreed to this because Shelley had said "LOOOR-a, Ralph cannot be alone at all, as he could fall and hurt himself. Please promise you'll be here with him the entire time." I could not promise this. I told Shelley I had other clients but that Ralph was the priority and I would spend every possible minute with him.

Shelley and Marty finally left after getting all their things into the town car and saying goodbye to Ralph, which included kisses and cuddles for about an hour.

I went to the room where I was staying and got back into bed. Ralph followed me and got into his bed, too. It was Friday morning and I had a full day's work in front of me but first, more sleep.

I woke up at 8 a.m. and began Ralph's lengthy morning routine, which included complicated food preparation, an exacting administration of all his meds and his morning walk. By 10:00 I was ready to leave and walk the dogs that could still walk.

I had hired out a few other jobs but still had the regular clients to walk, and one other pet-sitting job, which required visits but not sleepovers. This other particular job, which was going on at the same time as Ralph's, was for a woman who was high-maintenance.

She was "one of them;" a crazy cat lady who rescued cats, and she had a few dogs, too. She had flown to New Orleans to help rescue pets that had been orphaned during hurricane Katrina. She asked me for a discount on my services as she was a humanitarian and I gave it to her. This is before she returned from her trip and asked me if I had seen the jewelry she'd hidden from me because she couldn't remember where she hid it. I was mortified that she thought I would steal her jewelry, especially since she told me it was worthless but had sentimental value only.

She later called me and admitted she found the jewelry and apologized for thinking I might have taken it in the first place. She asked me if she could book me again because she was going back to New Orleans. I refused.

When she asked me if it was because of the jewelry incident I told her yes. I felt she didn't trust me and I was no longer comfortable being her pet sitter. She cried and told me the experience in New Orleans had been so emotional for her that she completely lost her judgment.

I did feel bad for her. She was a single woman living in West Hills in a house she had inherited from her mother. Her name was Kathy and while she had a good heart, she was a whack-job. I had reached this conclusion after she had guided me through her decent sized home to show me her cat masterpiece. Or "Caterpiece" as Kathy jokingly called it.

Kathy had sealed the Jacuzzi bathtub in her master bathroom and lined it with industrial strength plastic. She had then purchased a truck full of kitty litter and poured it into the tub creating the world's largest, shittiest cat box. "You can sit on the edge of the tub and scoop," she explained with pride. Somewhere her mother was spinning in her grave. While she was showing me her masterpiece two of her cats were in there taking a shit. One of them looked right at me. This is the difference between cats and dogs. A dog will not make eye contact in this position. Cats don't give a fuck.

"Always leave this window open," Kathy said as we left her bathroom and headed to the bedroom. "Obviously" I said back.

"You're welcome to sleep here you know," she told me, "if that makes things easier on you." If by "easier" she meant easier to die in my sleep from cat-hair asphyxiation, I'd pass.

I worked twice for Kathy. Her neighbors constantly checked on me, reporting to her all my comings and goings. I didn't appreciate this. Pet sitting is a two way trust street. I trust you don't have hidden cameras, and you have to trust I am doing my job. After the jewelry-hiding incident I never worked for Kathy again even though she called me from time to time to check my availability and say "hello." We both worked a lot in rescue and knew the same people, so I had to keep things cordial.

I went to Kathy's after I had left Ralph's and walked the morning dogs. I fed the cats and the dogs and scooped the litter bathtub. I went to the yard and picked up the dog shit and I brought in her mail. The house smelled so bad, it was difficult to stay in there too long. I wondered if she ever had anyone over. Probably not. Certain people, some people, but mostly women I have observed, become so involved with animals that their human relationships suffer. I was doubtful whether Kathy had had any sex in a while, at least not in her own house. I took out her garbage on the way out and drove to Woodland Hills. I was looking forward to getting back to Ralph and the comforts of his mansion.

The majority of my clients were in the Woodland Hills area near the Warner Center. I walked a few more dogs and got on the 101 to return to Ralph. It was still before dinnertime but Ralph greeted me as if he was hungry so I gave him some treats.

I sat in the recliner in Shelley and Marty's media room and enjoyed the air conditioner, happy to be relaxing. Ralph lay at my feet and I fell asleep for a few minutes. I was so tired, as being a busy pet sitter meant always being on the go and constantly running from place to place. I wanted to get up and take a shower but I could not muster the energy. Finally it was time for Ralph to be fed and then go for the walk before it got dark. The house phone rang next to the recliner, and I saw Marty's number on the caller ID. I answered the phone as I had been instructed. I hated answering the house phone when I was in a client's home as if I didn't answer they would think I wasn't there. Which truthfully, sometimes I wasn't.

"Call my cell phone," I would tell them.

"Answer the house phone if you see it's us," Marty instructed in his lawyerly voice. I said I would. Marty asked how Ralph was doing.

"Good!" I told him, "no problems." He told me they were in Hawaii now and would be in touch. And that I should call them if I needed anything or had any questions. I agreed.

Shelley had left me with an enormous amount of food in the kitchen. Most of the food was designated for Ralph, but some of it had been purchased with me in mind and some of it we could share such as the roasted chickens from the market. I needed a shower but I was also starving. I microwaved the chicken and looked in the freezer for some frozen veggies. I noticed there were dozens of prepared salads in the back of the fridge and decided to skip the frozen veggies and eat the blue cheese/cranberry salad with walnuts. I ate again in the media room and read Shelley's trashy celebrity magazines. It was hard to be concerned with all the crap going on in the world while sitting in this air-conditioned mansion.

I took my dishes to the sink, double-checked the alarm was set and padded down to my room. I stripped off my clothes and took a shower. I did not squeegee the stall when I finished. When I left the bathroom with my pajamas on Ralph was already snoring softly in his bed. "Goodnight, sweet prince," I said to him and then I got under the covers. I attempted to read a few pages of a book, but fell asleep thinking what I had to do tomorrow. At least it didn't involve getting up early. *Well, that depends on Ralph,* which was my last thought before I was out for the night.

Saturday morning I woke up to the bright sunshine coming through the window and Ralph's breath. He had been standing there breathing on me. Panting. "Okay boy, let's get you going." We went down to the kitchen and started with the feeding, the walking and the meds. I went back to my room and put myself together but Ralph didn't come with. I got dressed and went back to the kitchen to make myself a fancy coffee in their espresso machine. They had all the flavors and pods. There is a full bar too. They have so much stuff. Every room is over furnished. Art and pictures everywhere. Pictures of Ralph with the girls growing up are on the walls. There is an especially cute one of Ralph when he was a puppy with a graduation cap.

Ralph lay on the kitchen floor looking up at me. His tail did the slow up and down and he attempted to get up. "Ah, Ralph, buddy, don't get up on my account." I said. Shelley had pointed out all the places in the house Ralph liked to rest. This was one of them. "It's cool on the kitchen floor," Shelley had told me, "he likes that."

I went to the bar area near the media room and thought about making a bloody Mary. Whoever had designed this house was a very thoughtful person; putting the bar by the media room was a nice touch.

I just wanted to sit down and watch TV and veg out.

Shelley had left me these huge muffins and I selected the most blueberry-looking one and headed to a recliner.

It took forever to figure out the remotes and turn on the television. Marty had put together a comprehensive media usage guide to rival Shelley's Ralph-care guide but I didn't bother to look at it before pressing the "on" buttons on everything.

Finally, I managed to get a picture with sound. I felt pretty good about myself for figuring this out.

I got up and stretched, then walked through the house into the enormous dining room. The only table that fit in there is one you might use in a conference room. Even though it was the dining room, it sure looked like a conference room. I could picture Marty and Shelley with all their papers spread out everywhere, working on their cases side by side.

The length of the room was a picture window, overlooking green hills, trees, and a tiny bit of the golf course way out in the distance. I swung my arms out wide as I twirled and sang, "The hills are alive." I can't remember the rest of the song so I sing it again, "The hills are alive..." and suddenly I remember! "With the sound of music!" I twirl and sing imagining it was my house. I would never leave. I would seriously sing everything. And twirl and dance. This place is so awesome! I imagined twirling and dancing back in my apartment and envisioned myself knocking over bookshelves and walls. Not quite the same.

All the twirling got my heart rate up so I decided to sit down and finally watch some TV! Ralph was asleep when I passed him, his stomach and chest rising and falling steadily. I scrolled with the remote and discovered a whole category of movies just starting. I turned to the movie *"Constantine"* starring Keanu Reeves. I am excited by this choice.

I went back to the kitchen and poured a glass of mango juice. Really, this place is like staying at a hotel. I checked Ralph again and he was still sleeping. He raised his head while I passed him and watched me pass. I sat in the recliner and put my juice on a coaster. The movie started.

About halfway through the movie I put it on pause/mute because I needed to use the bathroom. I stop the frame. Constantine has a cigarette halfway to his mouth. His lips are parted in anticipation. He is looking towards the kitchen.

I walked out of the media room and passed Ralph to go to the bathroom. I stepped around him while looking down at him. His eyes were open and he was lying there, perfectly still. "Ralph," I said, "don't lie there looking like that, it makes it look…like… you… are… dead."

Then I realized Ralph really could be dead.

Suddenly I got on my knees besides Ralph. "Ralph!" I said touching his fur and looking at his eyes. He was not breathing and was staring out into space.

I put my head on his chest to see if I could hear a heart beat. There was none. I instantly knew he was gone and I burst into tears. I was overcome with grief.

"Ralph, Ralph, Ralph." I held him and I hugged him, wishing my tears would magically bring him back to life. I said a prayer for him sending him off to frolic over the rainbow bridge. I pictured Ralph as a puppy, playfully barking.

I couldn't believe he was dead, I needed a moment and so I paced the house. Why oh why did the dog have to die while I was in charge of watching him?

I didn't know what to do about calling Ralph's people. I felt awful. The wedding was that night and I didn't want to be responsible for ruining it. On the other hand, it was my responsibility to give them updates on Ralph and this was certainly an update.

I had gone from Julie Andrews in *The Sound of Music* to Meryl Streep in *Sophie's Choice*. I was tormented by the decision, what was the *right* choice?

I looked at the time. It was almost noon in Los Angeles, and still pretty early in Hawaii. Thinking I better get it over with or have to hang out with the dead dog all weekend, I picked up the house phone to call Shelley and Marty. I had to psych myself up to make the call. I poured a shot of vodka and gulped it down. I thought about waiting until tomorrow to tell them, at least that way the wedding would be over. But I decided against it.

Marty answered before the second ring. Taking a deep breath and steeling myself for his response I told Marty I had some difficult news for him.

"What's that?" Marty asked dryly. He was not friendly, and all business. I couldn't tell if he sensed what was coming next.

"I'm so sorry to have to tell you this but uhm, Ralph died," I said weakly, my voice rising into a squeak.

I felt almost giddy with inappropriate laughter, which is the body's response to emotional stress it's not handling well. I am failing at emotional stress.

Explosive diarrhea assembled in my intestines.

"How did that happen?" Marty asked, completely deadpan.

I had a lump in my throat the size of Mount Everest. I couldn't swallow. If I could have exchanged places with Ralph I gladly would have. I glanced over at him. I'd like to see him explain to one of Los Angeles' top attorneys how the pet sitter was dead. I'd like to see him do anything in fact, as I already missed him.

Caught off guard by Marty's question, my brain can only come up with, "he stopped breathing." And my brilliant follow up, "his heart went out."

"Uh huh," Marty said.

"Did you try CPR?" He asked, almost whispering.

I did not try CPR; I didn't think CPR would have worked in this case.

I took a Red Cross training class for pet first aid and so I do know dog CPR.

We all sat around in a circle in a room at the YMCA, and passed around a heavy dummy dog with black gums and a shiny nose. There isn't a way to seal a dog's mouth, so you can't do mouth-to-mouth on a dog. You have to do mouth to nose. The instructor demonstrated how to seal the dog's nose with your mouth and blow hard enough to inflate the fake dog's lungs. When you had done it correctly a bell would go off and the dog would start "breathing" again.

The instructor passed the phony pup to his right and we took turns blowing air into the fake dog's nose. Almost everyone got it on the first time. When the phony dog finally got to me I eyed it suspiciously. Probably about a dozen strangers had just wrapped their mouths around the dog's nose. I tried to be subtle about wiping it off with my sleeve.

I put my lips on the dog's slimy nostrils and blew. Nothing happened. I blew again. *Please work,* I thought over and over. *A dog's life might depend on it.*

Finally after heaving every last breath from my lungs into the dummy dog the alarm went off and the dog's lungs filled with fake air bringing him back to fake life. I looked around triumphantly. No one seemed particularly impressed.

I could tell by Marty's demeanor that he didn't want Shelley to find out just yet. I overheard her in the background laughing. They were probably drinking mimosas while overlooking the ocean, having a last minute fitting of the designer dresses they would wear tonight.

"What were you doing while this happened?" Marty asked me. I can't bring myself to tell him I was watching their high-definition television and drinking mango juice.

"I was uh, meditating."

"Where were you when you were meditating?" Marty asked as if I was on the witness stand.

"In my room, uh, the room, you know, the room I'm staying in. Sleeping in."

I felt awful about lying. At the time it seemed that telling Marty I was meditating would be the least offensive thing I could be doing while his dog was dying.

At that exact moment the mute button came undone on the TV and *Constantine* resumed at full blast, with Keanu Reeves yelling out something about the devil.

"What was that?" Marty asked.

As calmly as I could muster, I sprinted into the media room while muting Marty's hand held phone. I slammed my fingers down on all the remotes and the TV finally went off.

I returned to the phone and unmuted it, ignoring Marty's question. I told him I was so sorry and that Ralph had a wonderful morning.

"Tell me exactly what you did this morning with Ralph."

I told Marty everything about Ralph's morning, and he was silent. He asked me to hold on, as he needed to tell his wife and daughters. I didn't envy him. I pictured him walking through their spacious Hawaiian suite, with a look of dread on his face.

For what seemed like an eternity there was silence, followed by shrieking and wailing. It's as if Shelley is standing besides me and yelling. She is bawling "my baby, my baby, no, no, no." If there were anyway to undo this entire situation, I would have done it.

I'm pacing around the house now, avoiding the Ralph area.

"LOOR-a, it's Shelley, look it honey, he's not dead okay, he wouldn't do this to me, he's just in a trance, he does this sometimes. He's just really deeply sleeping." I couldn't tell if Shelley was trying to convince herself or me but I took another look at Ralph. I'm no doctor, but I was 99.9 per cent sure the dog is dead.

Possibly stiffening up, too. I don't mention this to Shelley.

"Okay," I said softly to Shelley. I will play her, "My Dog Isn't Dead," game.

"Take him to the vet," Shelley said. "Take him to the vet and the vet will know what to do." I immediately felt sorry for the vet.

I couldn't lift Ralph by myself. He seemed to have gotten heavier since he had died. The thought of dragging him through the house and out the garage and down the street to my car was unfathomable. What would the neighbors think? I would never get hired in this area again.

Leaving Ralph right where he took his last nap I went outside and pulled my car into the driveway.

All of a sudden Shelley's simple request wasn't that simple. I can't lift Ralph, he's too heavy and since he's not as cooperative as most dogs are when going to the vet, I can't get him into my compact car.

I called my friend Georgia. Georgia was studying for the bar; she'd taken it twice already and hadn't passed. I admired her perseverance and grit.

Georgia answered and asked what I wanted. She knew I wouldn't call her while she's in study-mode unless it was an emergency. I considered this an emergency and Georgia was a good friend. A little on the eccentric side but I didn't mind. I once saw Georgia add a fried chicken wing to a green smoothie she was blending.

"Gives it more protein."

She was "that" friend.

I explained to Georgia that I was pet sitting only the pet died. Georgia admitted that sucked. I told her I needed her help. Please, pretty please. I enticed her by telling her once she got to this house and saw what a good attorney's salary can buy she will definitely study harder and pass the bar this time. I practically guaranteed it.

Georgia came over. The guard gate called me to authorize her entrance. I told them to send her up. I was relieved to have Georgia with me. The house had gotten creepy since the dog died.

I saw Georgia as I was moving my car out of her way. I told her to park in the driveway so we could open the garage and move Ralph through there. Of course there was a Mercedes in all four of the garage spots so we had to use the driveway.

Georgia came in and looked around, letting out a soft whistle. "You weren't kidding."

I was giving Georgia the tour, walking her through the kitchen, when suddenly she spotted Ralph laying on the floor, only now he doesn't look like he's napping, he definitely looks dead.

"Aw shit" said Georgia. "I didn't want to see a dead dog today."

"Me neither." We hugged and cried over Ralph.

I grabbed a sheet from the linen closet and we moved Ralph into Georgia's van. Her back doors opened like an ambulance.

Driving over to the vet I asked Georgia if she thought I had any liability in this particular situation.

"There's always liability, Laura." She was not making me feel any better.

"You already sound like a lawyer," I told her and flipped over the sun visor for the mirror. I looked at my face. I looked awful. My eyes were swollen and puffy with mascara running everywhere. I tried to wipe some of it away but it wouldn't budge. Great, waterproof. How come waterproof mascara is waterproof but not tear proof?

I was planning on using the pool at Ralph's. Since Marty had asked me to continue to stay at the house, I suppose I still could, but I didn't feel like poolside lounging anymore.

THE PET SITTER'S TALE

Like a broken record, I repeated to Georgia over and over "I can't believe it, I can't believe it."

"I know, you can't believe it." Georgia was agitated and wanted to get back to her studies.

"Do you think I could have done anything to prevent this?" I asked.

"Yeah, you shouldn't have been watching such a crappy movie. Maybe *Constantine* killed him."

We remained silent until we arrived at the vet. I ran inside and grabbed a vet-tech. I told them who I was and asked if the vet would come out to the car. The vet came out right away. He had already heard from Shelley. Got an earful, I'm sure.

The vet was a kind man with a weathered face and a long stride. He reminded me of Robert Redford.

As we walked to the back of the van I told him what had happened.

"One minute he was napping and the next minute he was dead... well, I think he's dead."

The vet had been seeing Ralph for years. I opened the doors and there was Ralph. The sheet I had draped over him had slipped off and it looked like he was wearing a cape.

"Is he dead?" I asked tentatively, already knowing the answer.

The vet, god bless his heart, took one look at Ralph, looked at me and said,

"Yes dear, he's gone."

I started to cry some more. "Goodbye Ralph."

The shock had worn off, reality was settling in. The dog really was dead.

The vet left to go get a gurney. I stroked Ralph's head and told him he was a good dog.

When the vet returned with a gurney and another vet-tech I asked him if he could call Shelley and let her know. I didn't have the heart.

He said he'd do that; after all, it was part of the job. I asked him how he thought Ralph had died.

I needed closure.

The vet looked at me thoughtfully.

"Old age," he said, "living on borrowed time."

And then they wheeled Ralph away.

Dexter

# I Confess

It's not even six in the morning; I wake up before the alarm goes off. I used to be a late sleeper, enjoying sleeping past nine or even ten. Since I've been a pet sitter I've gotten accustomed to waking up early, hopping out of bed and beginning my day looking after other people's pets.

This morning I open my eyes slowly, I don't want to get up, my head still on the pillow and my eyes land right on the liquid chocolate eyes of my dog Dexter. Dexter's small head is on the pillow besides me. He is staring at me so sweetly. Dexter is a chiweenie; a dachshund and Chihuahua mix. He has a long body and a small head. He's not exactly attractive, certainly not my dream dog by a stretch but I love him fiercely. I stroke the top of his silky head, kiss him on his nose, and caress him. We lay besides each other snuggling. It's as if it is only the two of us in this world, this tiny island that is our bed.

"I love you, I love you so much." I say this out loud to Dexter, our heads sharing the same pillow. I say this to the dog as I stroke his shiny velveteen body and I mean it. It is true. Truer than true. I love the dog.

Then, like an unexpected, loud morning fart, the kind that wakes you up.

124

"I love you too."

Dexter's eyes widen and for a second I thought the words miraculously came from him.

I remember now, we're not alone in the bed. This "I love you" came from the masculine voice attached to the hairy backside just inches from mine. Caught in between asleep and awake, I had forgotten he was there. For one confusing second, I thought it was Dexter speaking. Dexter's ears perk up, we look at each other.

I was certainly NOT talking to *him*. Oh boy, I feel guilty, bad even. So bad. I wasn't expecting that, I forgot he was there. I wasn't talking to him. I swing my arm over my back and touch him, pat him gently and then I leave his side. I get up and let Dexter out and give him breakfast.

He thinks we just exchanged "I love you's."

I feel sad, everything's a mess. I love him, of course, I love him. Just not like the dog. I love the dog unconditionally even though he is an asshole sometimes and occasionally bites people. I am learning to love people unconditionally. Yearning to love *him* unconditionally. I think about our recent fight. Always a recent fight. A new hurt.

I know most people can relate to loving their dogs unconditionally. If people didn't care so much for their dogs I wouldn't have had a career for the last ten years. The dog has become the child you never had and the one relationship you haven't fucked up. At least from your dog's point of view, you are the perfect human being.

With some reflection and not too much at that, I know exactly what the roadblock is that prevents me from loving other people unconditionally. Not all people, just certain love interest. It's resentments. Resentments built up inside of me like piles of dog shit

125

in the yard. I know this isn't very Buddhist of me. I need to let these things go. I am not perfect. I am a work in progress.

I go over the recent argument between us, trying not to be resentful.

"What makes you think you can go to kickboxing, Laura? Huh? What makes you think you can do anything without asking me?" Pounds fist into palm. Yelling. We were in the bedroom, the end of a long day. Just telling each other about our days. Like, normal couples, I imagine. His reaction is so unexpected. The scary, sudden temper.

I sat on the bed. Back against the headboard. Legs crossed. Dexter jumps up into the spot for him in my legs, he settles himself in there. His safe burrow. We are watching him together, he's so mad now. Yelling. Dexter shakes a little. Loud noises scare him. Like the smoke alarm going off or ambulances passing by. Dexter was abused when he was a small puppy. Someone threw him out of an apartment window onto the street where he struggled to get up…while limping away from the apartment building; he was hit by a car. The driver of the car felt so bad that he took him to the nearest vet. The vet contacted the rescue and they agreed to perform life saving surgery if he would go to a forever home. No fosters. He had to get a home or they wouldn't perform the surgery. They called me. I said yes. I would take him sight unseen. Ten days later the rescue woman drove into my driveway. I saw her from my living room window; lifting Dexter out of the backseat, my heart lurched.

What had I committed myself to?

The Elizabethan Collar they put on him was so big it weighed his head down. He was a pathetic looking sack of bones with a satellite dish on his head. I wanted to shut the curtains and pretend I wasn't home.

The woman began to carry him towards my door. I opened the

door and walked out into the hot sun to meet them. We exchanged pleasantries quickly and I ushered them inside. Inside I had set up an exercise pen in my living room with pee-pee pads and blankets. There was water too. I wasn't sure what the food situation would be yet.

The woman put the dog down in the pen and he layed on his side panting. He looked awful. Skinny. I could see all his ribs. I asked if he was going to make it. She said he was having a difficult time. He needed rest and love and good care. He had metal pins put in his back legs and would always be limpy. Great, I have titanium rods in my back and now I have a dog with pins. Perfect.

His name wasn't Dexter then. It was Dover. I asked the lady if I could change his name. Dover is more suitable for a fish. Who names their dog Dover? I glance at the TV guide thingy on my table. Dexter! I will name him after a redheaded serial killer. And so it began.

I nursed Dexter back to health and he got better. Recovered. Became a good dog. Well, good-ish. Dexter has fear-aggression, which is left over from his first memories of being abused. Dexter has trust issues, too. Basically, Dexter bites people he doesn't know (on occasion) and ones he does know but doesn't like and sometimes he bites people he likes because he gets confused. He is great with other dogs but untrustworthy around people. I don't like it, I've tried to re-train him but at this point, I am kind of stuck with him. I committed to it and I am going to see it through to the end. Dexter is very loving and loyal to me and to my family.

My dream dog however is a golden retriever named Harley running along my beachfront property (since we're dreaming) with a red bandanna loosely tied on his neck. Harley has a big smile on his face as he runs towards me and jumps into my arms and licks my face.

But currently, my life is not my dream life. I am suddenly feeling the enormity of this. I need to make some changes. Just yesterday,

I crouched in the bathroom of my rental house trying to hide a dog with diarrhea from my landlord. The anxiety was turning my stomach into hot knots. The dog was spinning, she had to go. I can hear my landlord. An unexpected visit from him to check on a newly installed thermostat.

If he doesn't leave soon we are both going to shit ourselves. I put the dog in the tub. "Go in there if you need to," I tell her quietly. I pull down my pants and sit on the toilet. My stomach is ripped up. I cannot take this anymore. I've got to make the changes I need to make. Here are the things I want:

To live by the water, it doesn't have to be the ocean but it should be a large body of water, not a drainage pond. To drive a Maserati convertible, white please, I don't have to own the Maserati; a rental is fine, too. See Universe, I am being specific but flexible...or something better, right? And to sell my book and screenplay. I would like a nice, normal, loving relationship with someone who is not abusive or a psychopath. Oh yeah, I want to give a Ted talk, too. As a byproduct of all this success and happiness I will have more than enough money to open up an animal rescue or formal boarding facility. No more dog boarding in my house, I can't take this lifestyle anymore.

Even in my dreams I hear dogs barking and the phantom smell of dog urine permeates my every waking moment. Mornings after I wake up, sometimes even before I've had coffee, I do the poop-check. Poop check is literally walking around my house and looking for dog shit on the floor or carpet. Without fail, one of the dogs I've boarded has used the entire house as their bathroom. I feel like some fucked up version of the pet detective. I vow to write everyday and put some of these crazy dog stories down on paper. I'm going to get the life of my dreams, goddammit. The life of my dreams has less dog shit in it.

More yelling.

"I'm the best thing that ever happened to you Laura!" "You've made bad choices in the past and now admit it, I am the best thing that ever happened to you!"

"Say It!"

I sit on the bed with Dexter in my legs. He walks over and picks Dexter up and drops him on the carpeting a lot less gently than I would like but I don't say anything. This is getting ridiculous. "You can't hide behind the dog! You are going to have a conversation with me, I know you're capable of it because I hear you talking on the phone all the time to clients and friends."

"Say it! Say I am the best thing to ever happen to you!"

"I am the best thing to ever happen to you." I force a giggle when I say it.

I'm trying to deescalate the situation, demonstrate the ridiculousness of his statement. I'm constantly trying to deescalate situations and frankly I'm sick of it.

This infuriates him even more.

"You better knock it off Laura! You better knock it off or I'll…I'm not sure what will happen…do YOU understand?" I nod. I understand. Heart thumping.

I need to get out of this soul-crushing relationship before it becomes more than just soul-crushing. It is not too late for me. Do not talk back.

Dexter is tiptoeing back over to the bed. Quietly, he jumps back up and gets in between my legs again. I wonder if Dexter will bite him if he tries anything. I feel like Dexter might be trying to protect me but then again maybe he thinks I'm protecting him. Either way I feel better that Dexter is here. The man stomps around while yelling. Why should he stay with me if I love the dog more than him? Who else would want a woman only capable of loving dogs?

I stop answering the questions. Stop listening to them even. I can't hear his voice anymore. I am thinking about his accusations and I know in my heart that he's right about exactly one thing. I do love the dog more.

The dog is not a dick. The dog does not scream at me for insane reasons and as a matter of fact in the over ten years I have been in the dog business not one of these dogs has said a goddamn word to me. Not one word, not a single syllable. No mentions of looking tired or skin issues or a couple extra pounds. No asking me if I possibly could be moody because of menopause. Nope, the dog is silent. I definitely don't resent the dog.

The dog would never think of waking me up in the middle of the night to stick his penis in me because he can't sleep. No, in fact, the dog is pretty courteous like that. He doesn't get up unless I get up. The dog comes running to see me when I get home. Running! Can't wait to see me. Missed me so much and where have I been? The dog loves me unconditionally. Even if the dog had Facebook, which he does not, the dog would have the decency to log off when I come home and say hello.

I know it.

I think of how I used to be, of how I once felt: "Bubbly." That's how people would have described me at one time, a time that now seems long ago.

"Teary." Teary would be the most accurate description these days.

This has got to change.

I feel the sting of saltwater in my eyes. Try to blink it back. Lodged in my throat now, the dry sadness that cannot be swallowed. It is all too much. The tireless verbal abuse, the accusations, the threats. Each and every trouble, at my throat.

The heartless firing by one of my clients, right at Christmas, after I had worked for them for over ten years and then proceeded to humiliate myself by begging them not to fire me. I had only wanted to say goodbye to their dog, Ginger, one last time.

The almost unbearable death of Shana. Shana, the sweetest dog, and a client's dog that felt just like my own. I can still smell her fur. All my clients are starting to die or fire me and my boyfriend's an utter asshole. The depression is coming. My defenses are useless.

It's here now. The sadness. The heavy heart, I can't move.

Dexter puts his paw on me, looks up into my face.

Yes, I love the dog more.